MACK DADDY

MACK DADDY

Mastering Fatherhood Without Losing Your Style, Your Cool, or Your Mind

LARRY BLEIDNER

CITADEL PRESS
Kensington Publishing Corp.
www.kensingtonbooks.com

CITADEL PRESS BOOKS are published by

Kensington Publishing Corp.
850 Third Avenue
New York, NY 10022

Copyright © 2006 Larry Bleidner

All Kensington titles, imprints, and distributed lines are available at special quantity discounts for bulk purchases for sales promotions, premiums, fundraising, educational, or institutional use. Special book excerpts or customized printings can also be created to fit specific needs. For details, write or phone the office of the Kensington special sales manager: Kensington Publishing Corp., 850 Third Avenue, New York, NY 10022, attn: Special Sales Department; phone 1-800-221-2647.

CITADEL PRESS and the Citadel logo are
Reg. U.S. Pat. & TM Off.

First printing: April 2006

10   9   8   7   6   5

Printed in the United States of America

Library of Congress Control Number: 2005934017

ISBN 0-8065-2703-X

To my father, Walter.
Though I often shut my eyes,
he showed me true North;
and so the course is never long obscured.

And to Irene who made me a dad—
enabling me to know the two joys of the universe,
my daughters Olivia and Jackie.

CONTENTS

CHAPTER 1

CHAPTER 4 (1–3 Months)

CHAPTER 5 (3–12 months)

CHAPTER 6 (1–3 Years)

CHAPTER 7 (3–6 Years)

CHAPTER 8 (School)

CHAPTER 9

EPILOGUE

MACK DADDY

Chapter 1

The Big, BIG Picture

Daddy.

Close your eyes and say the word.

What happens?

Do you smile and see the best guy you know?

Do you cringe and try to think of something else?

A long, long time from now, when your adult child thinks of you, what will fill his or her heart?

Dad. It's *the* most common job. Yet for prestige, it trumps CEO, CFO, and all the other meaningless ee-eye-ee-eye-ohs. It beats Rock Star, Movie Star, President, Premier, Emperor, you name it. It pays better than all of them combined.

When you're an old man dozing in the sun, will you reminisce about that big account? That lawsuit you wish would go away? Superbowl XXXVIII?

Perhaps, if you're a fool.

A wise man remembers a toddler's arms around his neck and a small voice calling the sweetest word in the universe.

"Daddy."

The Annunciation

She's pregnant.

Hopefully, that's good news to you both. But even if you've been planning for it and are ready emotionally, financially and otherwise, you'd be an idiot not to feel at least a bit apprehensive.

Relax. You can hack it. Only a few billion guys have done it before you.

Of course, *you* are a cut above, and expect more of yourself. You want to be a stellar, spectacular, magnificent dad. A MACK DADDY.

And so you shall.

Being a MACK DADDY is mostly about attitude. There's a lot of claptrap and propaganda out there. Television tells us that dads are pot-bellied, polyester-wearing buffoons lacking the brains to blow hot soup. Obsolete sperm donor/oafs. You've done your job, now let MOM take over!

Yeah, right.

First, get your mind around two basic truths.

1. *She's* pregnant, *you're* not.

   "We're pregnant" is a *moronic* catch phrase, probably coined by some imbecile/non-parent chick-flick screenwriter.

   Over the next nine months, *we* won't be puking, swelling, craving, waddling, gobbling prenatals, pawed by OBGYNs— *she* will. And *we* won't be spending 12, 24, maybe 36 hours trying to pass something that feels like a break dancer in a razor-wire suit.

There's no *I* in TEAM.

No *WE* in PREGNANT, either.

2. You are *needed* . . . now more than ever.

When she first tells you she's pregnant, she'll dash through an emotional gauntlet. So, the word of the moment is *reassurance*.

She may be thinking: *Will I gain a ton and never lose it? Will my hair fall out? Will I get acne? Varicose veins? A nasty Caesarian scar? Swollen ankles? Will my boobs fail the pencil test? The laptop test? Does this ruin any possibility of my ever becoming a Laker Girl/Playmate/Victoria's Secret model?*

Fling some names in her face.

Cindy Crawford. Pamela Anderson. Reese Witherspoon. Catherine Zeta-Jones. Demi Moore. Elle MacPherson. Jennifer Connelly. Brooke Burke.

All moms. All smokin'. And of course, your wife is hotter than any of them.

Take her to dinner—that night—at some romantic eatery. While there, tell her how hot she looks and plan a couple of long weekends away or a vacation before the baby arrives. If possible, do it before the third trimester.

This endeavor will take both your minds off anxieties (all of which are unfounded) and put this best of all possible occurrences in the proper context—a *celebration*. Because what she's cooking in her belly will give you more laughs and kicks than you can possibly imagine. Like sex, downhill skiing, and sport fishing, there's no explaining it . . . you just have to see for yourself.

It's surprising how quickly the whole maternity drill starts. Morning upchucks may commence as soon as a week after conception. If she's hurling, offer to hold her hair out of her face. (Turned off? Don't be a girly-man! Gut it out—you've done worse on a dare.).

Wow and amaze her with this little-known trick. While she sleeps, place a glass of water and some Saltines on her nightstand. The moment she awakens, have her munch a few. It usually quells nausea. Ginger tea works okay, too.

Be there. She may prefer to barf in private. Fine, give her her space. But stand outside the door and ask if she's okay every now and then. It's the Mack Daddy thing to do.

The cravings will kick in pretty soon, too. My wife's was watermelon. Lucky we live in Southern California. If hers is pork roll and you live in Dubai . . . you're screwed!

Whatever it may be, buy bulk.

Why MACK DADDIES? Why Now?

Fathers are almost invariably depicted by Madison Avenue and Hollywood as buffoons. In sitcom land, dad is typically an unkempt slob, who comes home from work, cracks open a domestic beer, flops on the couch, scratches his balls, and clicks a remote unit until he falls asleep.

Mom is always trim, sexy, and basically tolerates Dad while she raises the family, brings home the big bucks, and pops off punch lines with the cadence of a Vegas comic.

The kids ridicule him. He's never hip, cool, kind, or wise. No, Dad is an asshole.

What other group would tolerate such relentlessly negative portrayal by the media? What network would dare lampoon women, gays, blacks, Latinos, Asians, or any ethnicity?

What makes the networks and ad agencies think it's open season on fathers? Would it take Freud to posit that perhaps the miscreants writing this shit are the offspring of pathetic losers—which shaped their twisted renderings of fathers?

My dad was a very cool guy. So were my grandfathers and my uncles. All my friends' dads were okay, too. Why is every dad on *Lifetime* an abusive, drunken bastard, so dangerous to his family that mommy must get a *restraining order*?

The dad-dissing is everywhere. Here's an insightful piece that appeared in the *Washington Post*, penned by my friend and exemplary MACK DADDY, Bill McGee.

Mothers, Mothers Everywhere—and Nary a Plug for Dad
By William J. McGee
(Washington Post)

I've been a single dad for most of the 11 years of my son's life, so you might think *I'd* have gotten over feeling slighted when men are left out of the child-raising talk. I believed I'd gotten over it—until I came across a poster touting Crown Theatres' new "Movies for Moms" (yes, that's a trademarked phrase), exhorting mothers to "Bring your baby to the movies!" Then I discovered that Loews Cineplex offers a "Reel Moms" program ("Stroller check is available; admission for grown-ups is regular ticket price, babies are free").

The Loews fine print acknowledges that some of those grown-ups may be fathers, but I couldn't help feeling excluded even as I realized that many other caregivers probably wouldn't care. Like other major retail organizations, Crown and Loews clearly aren't worried about offending 50 percent of the parenting pool. After all:

• When it comes to peanut butter, "Choosy Moms Choose Jif."
• Kix cereal is "Kid-Tested, Mother-Approved!"
• Robitussin is "Recommended by Dr. Mom."

- Kari Lee's cookie mix is "a mix that moms and kids love."
- The BIC Evolution coloring pencil is "for kids . . . but moms will love it too!"
- And the American Dairy Association warns: "Hey Moms! Don't forget the power of cheese."

I probably don't need to remind you that single dads, custodial dads, and just plain-old dads also purchase peanut butter, breakfast cereal, cough syrup, cookies and even pencils. Heck, I've even been known to buy cheese.

But I've given up expecting media recognition for Dads' efforts. Just look at the contents of *Parenting* magazine: "The Mom Guide," "Moms Dish on How They Handle Misbehaving Kids," "How Moms Decide," "Embarrassing Mom Moments" and "Mom-Tested Secrets."

Now, you might be thinking that I'm suffering from a mild case of hypersensitivity. But generalizations like these affect the way we view both men's and women's roles—in an office, on a battlefield and in a courtroom. Terms excluding women have largely—and thankfully—gone away. Politicians and broadcasters now praise our "service-men and— women overseas" or "the men and women of the police department." Women are acknowledged for roles traditionally undertaken by men.

But the reverse is not true.

Admittedly, there are plenty of fathers who perpetuate this. I once worked with a publisher who complained of having to spend the weekend "baby-sitting" his kids. How, I asked him, is it possible to baby-sit your own children?

Hollywood and advertisers often show moms struggling with the dual challenges of home and career, and in the movies that do portray men in nurturing roles, prepare for high jinks! Nothing generates laughs like a guy changing a diaper. (Witness *The Pacifier*, in which Vin Diesel holds a bare-bottomed baby over a toilet bowl.)

Is it any wonder that it's so hard to find changing tables

in men's rooms? Is it any wonder that so many judges consistently fail to recognize the rights of fathers in family courts?

Anyone who has spent time in family court can testify that there are plenty of terrible parents of both genders. But in a lot of courtrooms, fathers are seen as little more than the keepers of the checkbooks. (I recently Googled "deadbeat dad" and got 61,900 results; "deadbeat mom" returned just 5,030.)

Memo to Hollywood and the advertising world: I'm one of many caring dads out there. And I'm quite choosy, too. I just won't be choosing Jif.

If Bill's article strikes a chord, read on and join up. You're one of *us*.

Archetypes

Women get tons of help prepping for parenthood—clinics, support groups, friends, books, magazines, older sisters, mothers.

What do men get?

Have a cigar!

The dad thing is new. Maybe you need a little direction. Have a look at some typical father templates, then choose a type.

Your choice will be determined by how much you want to be involved raising your kid. Ideally, it's a 50-50 split with Mom. Of course, the ratio fluctuates but it shouldn't be too unbalanced.

Here's the basic menu:

Daddy Distant

This guy has been immortalized in story and song from Charles Dickens to Harry Chapin to Pearl Jam. Usually a workaholic, he justifies absentee fatherhood by pointing to a lush college fund, large home, and the latest and greatest . . . stuff. (His kid, however, might have difficulty pointing out Dad in a lineup.)

Not always a corporate mogul, sometimes he just doesn't want to deal. He doesn't do diapers. He doesn't do feedings. He doesn't read bedtime stories. He doesn't realize he's raising a stranger.

Lactating Daddy

He says, "We're pregnant." He wears bib-overall cargo pants bulging with baby paraphernalia. His wife is behind the wheel and he's in the backseat pretending to nurse. He consults daily with schoolteachers to make sure little Octavius isn't behaving too aggressively. He runs monthly stool samples to the lab to be certain baby's digestion is up to par. His house is so goddamn childproof, it looks like a rubber room. Junior *must* wear a safety helmet—even when sleeping—because you just can't be too careful!

By the time his kid is in college, Lactating Daddy will be starting *man-opause.*

Rubber-Stamp Daddy

Although involved, he defers to Mom on every issue.

Sure, Mom has maternal instincts. Who says they trump paternal ones?

We've all seen couples where Daddy defers to Mommy on every child-rearing issue. And the mommy is an archetype, too, determined to raise a male or female sissy. That's sissy, not *gay*. There are countless lionhearted gays. But a sissy, whether gay or straight, male or female, is a doomed pariah, for this is a person motivated solely by fear.

She inculcates her five-year-old with her dog phobia by scooping him into her arms and fleeing from yappy poodles as if they were Godzilla. She cradles his head as if fractured because he was splashed in a kiddie pool. She runs him to the hospital to get a scraped knee x-rayed. She transfers him from nursery school because some kid bullied him. She cuts his food because "knives are dangerous." Where is daddy? He's her enabler, helping her get away with this disgusting and ruinous behavior.

Der Fuehrer Daddy

Polar opposite of Rubber-Stamp Daddy, it's his way or the highway. Typified by Captain von Trapp of *The Sound of Music*, this martinet makes kids goose-step before they can crawl. His kids are perfect—never a behavior problem. Until they go away to school, where they promptly OD on heroin or are murdered in a bar fight. Why? Because they've been leashed so tight, they have no idea how to behave when free.

Fuehrer Daddies commit a terrible sin. They deprive children of childhood.

They don't necessarily wear jackboots and carry a riding crop. Sometimes they wear a windbreaker that says COACH.

MACK DADDY

He might wear a tool belt and drive a pickup. He might wear a five-thousand-dollar suit and be driven in a limo. But above all else, know this: He loves his kid and his kid *loves* him.

MACK DADDIES are serene. Confident. Self-possessed. When his kid trips in the playground and scrapes a knee, of course he picks him up and comforts him. But he lessens the duration of wailing by examining the scraped knee and laughing. "Look at that, Joey! That gash looks like Grandma (fill in in-law's name)'s nose!"

He'll heft Joey like a ditty bag, and humming a sea chantey, take him to the water fountain, where he'll fill his mouth and clean the wound by spraying it like a pachyderm.

I witnessed a guy do exactly that. By the time he finished spraying Joey's knee, several other smiling toddlers were lined up for the same treatment. Their moms looked like they were hoping for a spraying, too.

MACK DADDY is the one to be. Cool, calm, and collected, he's the go-to guy in every situation.

Distant Daddy misses junior's school play because he's at the office finishing the Zimzow report. MACK DADDY finds some subordinate to finish his report for him, so he's at that auditorium clapping wildly.

Lactating Daddy bolts his four-year-old into a roll-caged Volvo and drives white knuckled. MACK DADDY puts the convertible top down and sits his kid on his lap, letting him "drive" into the garage.

Rubber-Stamp Daddy watches Mommy frantically screaming at Junior to stay away from the filthy salmonella-carrying turtle. MACK DADDY helps his kid feel the shell, the pointy claws, and the wrinkly skin. Then he helps his kid wash his hands before they scarf down meatball heros.

Der Fuehrer Daddy chains his tone-deaf daughter to the Steinway for an hour a day. MACK DADDY exposes his daughter to music, dance, art, and athletics and sees what interests her.

Making an Informed Decision

Perhaps you're still unsure about which dad archetype suits you best. All have their benefits. Here are some top-ten lists that may help you choose a role model.

TOP TEN REASONS IT'S GOOD TO BE LACTATING DADDY

10. You never get sand kicked in your face at the beach—bullies assume your wife is the man.

9. When your kid is old enough to ask, *Why do men have nipples?* you can whip out a boob and squirt his face.

8. Guys will give you their seats on a crowded bus or subway.

7. You drink free on ladies night.

6. If you get fired, you can catch up on your soaps.

5. You can watch chick flicks and feel comfortable blubbering.

4. Air kissing gives you a chance to rub up against some great racks.

3. Your kid need never get involved in those *my daddy can beat up your daddy* arguments.

2. MILF's find you non-threatening, making them easy prey.

1. Breast pumps can produce hands-free orgasms.

TOP TEN REASONS IT'S GOOD TO BE DADDY DISTANT

10. The closest you ever get to a shitty diaper is watching some TV mom change one on a commercial.

9. Sleep deprivation is not a part of your life, unless the bimbo you picked up at the hotel bar wants a replay.

8. You'll never have to endure the horror of a performance of *Annie*.

7. Neighbors think you're the sexy, single uncle from out of town (Or maybe the *funny* uncle they tell their kids to avoid).

6. Unsullied by drool or gakked formula, your cashmere pullovers last forever.

5. You never have to scrape a lollipop off the seat of the Alfa.

4. Since you are never seen in public with your kids, that sexy Starbucks barrista babe won't guess that you're the same age as her dad.

3. It's better to be thought stylish and maybe gay than dumpy and definitely straight.

2. If/when you do spend time with the kids, they're *damned* grateful!

1. When you dress as Santa at Christmas, you won't need to disguise your voice—or face.

10. If the baby spews on you, no problem. Just throw on a fresh uniform.

9. It's good to be called "Sir," even if only by your children.

8. You save on Halloween candy—neighborhood kids avoid "that psycho's" house.

7. Outings with the baby are a snap—you can hang all the paraphernalia from the D-rings on your fatigues.

6. Who needs hugs when you can get salutes instead?

5. Free shoe shines for life—from the kids.

4. You need never endure boring small talk. Nobody talks to you at all.

3. Your pro sports franchise wardrobe assures you admittance to the fanciest establishments—through the service entrance.

2. Goose-stepping is aerobic, keeps hamstrings limber, and really sets you apart from those other jogging fools.

1. If they make *Taxi Driver II*, you can double Travis Bickle.

Still trying to find your footing in the world of dads? Below is a compendium of entries culled from thousands of college yearbooks and cross-tabbed with archetypical dads. If you see some of yourself in these guys, it may help you on your path to self realization.

The Yearbook Test

LACTATING/
RUBBER-STAMP

DISTANT

MACK DADDY

DER FUEHRER

A

MAJOR: Military Science

ACTIVITIES: Grecco-Roman wrestling, Paint Ball Squad, Chess Club, Thule Society, Crew (U-Boat)

HOBBIES: Civil War Reenactment Peloponnesian War Reenactment, Hundred Years War Reenactment

FAVORITE QUOTATION: *Smash their heads*
—Genghis Khan

B

MAJOR: Women's Studies

ACTIVITIES: Peer Helper Network, Spring-Fest Committee Co-Chair, Drama Club, Glee Club, Feminist Majority Leadership Alliance, Dance Club, W.H.A.P (Women Who Administer Punishment)

HOBBIES: Hentai. Sailor Moon, Slash Fiction

FAVORITE QUOTATION: *I am Sailor Moon, the champion of justice. In the name of the moon, I will punish you!* —Sailor Moon

C

MAJOR: Business Administration

ACTIVITIES: Tyro Tycoon Club, Delta Sigma Pi, Alpha Kappa Psi, Future Business Leaders of America, Golf, Miniature Golf, Investment Club

HOBBIES: Collecting corporate mission statements.

FAVORITE QUOTATION: *To create a vision of*

core value principles with added value,
passion, customer focus and stuff.

—My personal Mission Statement

D

MAJOR: English Literature
ACTIVITIES: Tai Kwan Do, Paris-Dakar
Rally, Polo, Capt., Fencing Team, 12-
Meter Race Team, Biathlon, Iditarod
HOBBIES: Pre-Columbian Art, Luthier,
Ragtime Piano, Spearfishing,
Metaphysics, Lycanthropy, Chemin de
Fer
FAVORITE QUOTE: *Is that all there is?*

—Peggy Lee

Answers: (A) Der Fuehrer (B) Lactating/Rubber-Stamp (C) Distant
(D) MACK DADDY

Know Thyself

If you're still unsure about which archetype dad you'd prefer to
be, here's a multiple choice quiz that may help you determine
which best fits your style.

My favorite movie is
  a. *Three Weddings and a Funeral.*
  b. *IBM Employee Orientation* video.
  c. *Triumph of the Will.*
  d. *Goldfinger.*

My favorite song is
  a. "My Heart Will Go On" (theme from *Titanic*).
  b. "Leavin' On a Jet Plane."
  c. "Horst Wessel Song."
  d. "In the Summertime" (by Mungo Jerry).

People are really impressed when I
   a. pick up my kid and spin so fast, my caftan swirls like a
      dervish's.
   b. text-message my eight-month-old from the Monday-morning
      meeting.
   c. show them my NHL all-star athletic cup collection.
   d. twirl a plate on a cue stick—with my toddler sitting on the
      plate.

I believe in
   a. Goddess.
   b. the company mission statement.
   c. my right to harbor homoerotic thoughts while viewing
      Master and Commander, Top Gun, or *Rudy.*
   d. Bob Mitchum, Sam Kinison, and Tony Montana.

My greatest regret is
   a. not TiVo-ing each and every episode of *Rosie.*
   b. Missing the eBay IPO.
   c. Not snipping a lock of Woody Hayes's hair while stalking
      him.
   d. Not downshifting in the final turn at the '99 LeMans.

In my wallet, I keep a photo of
   a. Andrea Dworkin.
   b. Jack Welsh.
   c. me—arms akimbo, atop the Brandenburg Gate.
   d. my kids.

SCORING: For each (a) answer, give yourself one Lactating/Rubber-
Stamp Daddy point. For each (b) answer, one Daddy Distant
point. Each (c) answer, one Der Fuehrer Daddy point. Each (d)
answer, one MACK DADDY point.

Which Daddy Will You Be?

A MACK DADDY's kids are his reason for living. And while you're out world-beating to provide all the tangible necessities or luxuries of life, don't fail to render the most important nourishment of all—love. Being there when that child needs you—with open arms and heart, will do more to ensure his or her happiness and success than anything else you could possibly provide.

Of course, some of those other dads would disagree with the above. Especially those dads (and plenty of moms, too) who view the child as *accessory*.

You see them all the time, especially in high-income urban and suburban areas. Kids that are conceived, born, and raised with the same ennui reserved for any other material acquisition. And with gene mapping, it won't be long until they can be ordered with all the options you desire.

I witnessed the following tableau one morning at my daughter's nursery school. Fortunately, she's very outgoing and generally skips into the classroom with nary a backward glance. I hung around to watch a scene unfold with a little kid named Tyler, who wasn't so eager for the learning experience.

Tyler's dad is an LA cliche. It's Casual Friday, so he wears his French blue shirt sans cravat. His three-button charcoal Armani AX suit and downsized, quasi Doc Martens tell us he's "industry" or industry wannabe.

Little Tyler is distraught. Wanting to be held, he reaches his arms up to Execu-dad (a sub-species of Daddy Distant). But Execu-dad does not hug. He's in mid to upper management now, and hugging's just not . . . *appropriate*. Besides, this is a great time to sharpen his people skills.

As Tyler's little fists clench Execu-dad's leg in a death grip, Execu-dad looks down at his 3 ½ year-old son and demands, "What's the problem here?"

The kid murmurs something unintelligible and buries his tear and snot-streaked face in the old man's thigh.

Spotting effluvium on his worsted-gabardine trousers, Execu-dad's nostrils flare with fury. His eyes blink rapidly as he tries to recall some anger-management dialogue from that Human Resources seminar.

Through clenched teeth he hisses, "Help me to understand what is going on here, Tyler."

And I'm thinking, *that's not exactly it, pal. The canned HR phrase you meant to regurgitate was, I think, "help me to help you."*

Tyler looks at him imploringly, but Execu-dad is focused on his besnotted slacks. His mind works under his Joe Rogan hairdo, coiffed to camouflage his lengthening driveways.

How will I look like Master of the Universe at the 10:30 staff meeting with snot on my leg? Do I have time to run home and change and still make the meeting?

Execu-dad uncoils the kid's arms from around his leg as the boy continues to quietly weep.

"Just get in there," Execu-dad commands as he shoves his weeping son through the door.

Tyler stumbles into the room with tear-blurred vision and bursts into full-blown sobbing. He crouches in a corner and cries into his folded arms.

Execu-dad shakes his head as his face says, *How did such weakness spring from my loins?*

He spins on his heel, unholsters his phone, and flips it open like Captain Kirk summoning Star Fleet Command. Then he strides off purposefully to his masterofmycubicle job, secure in the knowledge that he has once again "managed" a situation.

While surely a sad scene for Tyler, it was a graphic depiction of a Daddy Distant in action.

How would those other dads have handled it?

- Der Fuehrer Daddy would have had Tyler shot for cowardice.
- Lactating Daddy would have whisked Tyler away to an emergency session at his therapist's.
- Rubber-Stamp Daddy would have just called Mom on the cell for instructions.
- MACK DADDY would have hugged and kissed the fear right out of Tyler, then walked him through the door and hung with him until he was okay.

Plenty of mommies also view child as accessory. Some time ago, I was acquainted with a businesswoman who held a mid-six-figure job with a multinational company. Her hefty salary was basically fun money, because her investment-banker husband made a mid-*seven*-figure income.

By the time she wanted to become a mom it was too late. (Another victim of Helen Gurley Brown's *You Can have It All* scam. Nobody gets it all—male or female, there's always a price.) So, she decided to adopt. After months of bureaucratic red tape and tens of thousands of dollars, she adopted a beautiful child. Congratulations!

After a maternity leave (hmmm . . . okay, no need to split hairs), she . . . *went back to work!* And the baby went . . . *into day care!*

Was that baby an adoption? Or an acquisition?

The Physical MACK DADDY

If your waistline equals your inseam, if you never lose your breath, and can bench-press double your weight, skip ahead. But if you resemble an R. Crumb character more than a Frazetta, pay attention.

Too busy making the big bucks to get in shape? Okay, die young. Your kid's stepfather will be very grateful for the inheritance.

He'll probably blow a wad on a home gym so he doesn't wind up like you.

MACK DADDIES, while never fops, *do* take pride in their appearance. Nobody expects you to look like Mr. Olympia. But do you really want to look like the Michelin man?

Seven Magic Letters

Each year, hundreds of scam artists write diet books with algorithmic formulae for caloric intake. Then they hustle calculators, food scales, and expensive nukeable low-cal dinners. It's all crap.

An *honest* diet book could be written on one page, with seven letters.

E-A-T L-E-S-S

Unless you're a lumberjack or sumo wrestler, eat a *light* breakfast. The more you eat, the hungrier you'll be at lunch. What's light? Grapefruit and toast. Bowl of oatmeal. Cheerios. Forget all that nonfat milk, artificial sweetener, and dry toast nonsense. It's the big stuff that kills you.

In L.A., where everybody is shallow and sexy, you'll see an interesting thing: hot, wasp-waisted babes toting huge bottles of designer water. (Some even carry them in kinky-looking, little fishnet strappy slings.)

Those 6 percent body-fat vixens know something—water can fool a belly into thinking it's full of pizza. When you get ravenous between lunch and dinner, gulp some H_2O. Then reach for an apple, orange, or other fruit. Trail mix is okay, too.

Stay the hell away from pasta, pizza, cheesecake, and so on. If it looks fattening, it is.

Timing is key. Remember this axiom: *Nothing big after six.* When you chow down late it turns right into blubber. Eat a reasonable dinner as early as possible. Then, before bed, knock down a bowl of Cheerios. That'll keep you feeling full until morning.

Another tip: booze. Whether beer, wine, or grain alcohol, booze helps make and keep you fat. A coupl'a pops on the weekend is fine. But booze actually inhibits the burning of fat, making it impossible to shed weight while drinking.

In time, your stomach will shrink. You will be less hungry. Your pants will swim on you. You'll need to add notches to your belt. That hottie in Marketing will take an interest in you. We'll stop there.

When my first daughter was born, I was about 30 pounds overweight. Suddenly, longevity was really appealing. My wife got to work on me (and I on myself), and within a year, I had lost all 30 and my cholesterol and blood pressure were (to quote my doctor) at Olympian levels. It can be done.

A final thought: No need to get anal about diet or exercise. We all know guys who would pass up hot oil wrestling with the Laker Girls because *Hey, man, it's Wednesday—I work arms and shoulders tonight*. There's a word for these guys—morons. Ditto with the food. If you've been careful all week and feel like ingesting and entire lasagna on Saturday, why not? You've earned it.

The MACK DADDY Workout

Ask any pro body builder—the look is 80 percent diet. You can spend five hours a day at the gym, and if you don't eat properly, you'll just be a strong fat guy.

If you dig gyms, join one. If you can't get in a good workout in 50 minutes, either the gym's too crowded or you're wasting time bullshitting with other patrons. Three or four times a week should do it.

It's all about consistency. First, cardio—a mile or two on a treadmill (with some degree of incline) and a mile or two on a bike should get your heart pumping. Then, some sit-ups (or crunches) if you prefer. In the weight room, the basics are bench press (or dips), preacher curls, leg presses, or lunges. Form is critical.

If your personal trainer doesn't look fantastic he may be a fraud—nobody licenses these people and many are clowns.

Some bodybuilders actually write books that are full of counterproductive nonsense. The best one I ever read was by Franco Columbu. His program worked and, as a chiropractor, he was above all concerned with avoiding injury. Franco has a website (www.colombu.com) and several books in print.

MACK DADDY Mythbuster

"No Pain, No Gain" is bullshit. If you injure yourself working out, you *will* have pain, and gain nothing. Take it slow, always warm up, and if you don't know what you're doing, get help from someone who does.

Think tortoise and hare with weight loss and training. Slow and steady will make you a winner.

Not a gym rat? If you don't need coconut biceps, you can get toned, trim, and very strong with running and calisthenics.

Fatherhood is a challenge—one that demands strength, stamina, and agility. But doesn't life demand the same?

The Metaphysical MACK DADDY

You've chosen a role model. You have a nutritional and workout regimen. Let's work on your outlook.

MACK DADDY MANTRAS

1. TV and movie dads are assholes. I am superior to them.

2. I would not leap on a live grenade for my kid . . . for my kid, I would *eat* one.

3. Sometimes Mom knows best.

4. Sometimes *I* know best.

5. My kid will grow fast and split. I'll spend every second I can with him/her.

6. I'll keep myself in top condition. My kid deserves an able dad—for life.

7. I'm my kid's hero. I will never give him reason to believe otherwise.

8. I will expose my kid to the Three Stooges. (If mommy objects, see #4.)

9. My kid is unique and not my clone. I will help him/her find his bliss.

Anxiety Control

Life with your kid will be like a video game. The moment you slay one ghoul, a fresh one pops up to replace it.

MACK DADDIES don't have it any easier than those cringing, bet-wetting, neurotic nail-biting fathers. They just handle the problems a whole lot better.

A few thoughts.

Nothing is forever. The moment you juggle bottles, nipples, and formula like a circus performer, your kid will start on solid food, and you'll be packing away all the bottle paraphernalia for the next birth. By the time you figure out whether she digs Gerber or Beechnut strained bananas, she'll be tearing into the spare ribs you brought home from the Golden Pagoda. You just can't keep up.

So get Zen . . . today.

When the baby comes, follow your nose. What do I mean by that? Infants are all born with a similar smell. It has something to do with being marinated in placenta for the better part of a year. It's kind of like talcum powder or baby oil—whose manufacturers are trying to fabricate that natural, incredible, inimitable odor. God put it there for an insidious reason. Babies can be stress machines. They can drive you nuts, no question. They are utterly defenseless. So, they are made irresistibly cute—soft, pudgy, cooing, gurgling—to offset their less attractive qualities. One big gun in their arsenal of cute is that smell. It doesn't last. By about three months, it's almost gone.

Grab your baby. Bury your nose in her neck, belly, or crook of her fat little arm and *inhale*. Chanel would pay anything to be able to reproduce that odor.

When our child was an infant and I'd get tense, my wife would say, "Go hold your daughter." If she was awake, I'd do that. If she was asleep, I'd lean into the crib and push my nose into her neck. That scent produced instant calm better than a jigger of Jack. Try it. It works.

Don't "box with ghosts." Fight those video ghouls as they pop up. If you feel knocked down, take the ten-count—nobody's watching. Everything will work out. Your son or daughter will grow up beautifully—he'll be fed, clothed, housed, and educated, and then . . . he'll be gone.

Breathe.

Cool Facts About Some MACKIN' DADDIES

Which states are home to the most fecund fathers? The top five are Utah, Texas, Arizona, California, and New Mexico. (The lowest are Maine, Vermont, West Virginia, Pennsylvania, and New Hampshire.)

However, while we mass produce silicon chips and Chevys, when it comes to kids, we're low volume manufacturers compared to other countries.

Top five nations for fertility are Niger, Mali, Uganda, Afghanistan, and Chad. The United States ranks 156 out of 223, with Germany and China at the bottom.

Box car numbers, while interesting, always pale beside more personal stats. Here are some eye-poppers from dads who really, really *got busy:*

- In Arabia, King Saud produced about 80 kiddies by 20 wives.
- In Kenya, a guy named Akuku has been married more than 100 times (but divorced only 30) and figures he's made around 160 babies (though he's not exactly sure).
- At its zenith, the empire established by MACK DADDY Genghis Kahn covered more of the planet than any before or since. He kicked ass and subjugated every nation from Japan (through Russia, Persia, and Iraq) to Poland. All that conquest can wind a warrior up pretty tight, so GK had some 500 wives and concubines bivouacked for stress relief. How many kids did the mighty Mongol father? Smock-wearing geeks who track chromosomes and gene pools estimate that 0.5 percent of humankind can trace its ancestry to Genghis. Hands (or maybe pants) down, he gets the grand prize for best multitasking MACK DADDY.

Have a *THUNDERSTORM!*

Fact: Seconds after you popped the question to your wife, her pals were planning her bridal shower, a custom that includes stupid hats, dildos, vibrators, and displays of estrogen-soaked, ersatz sentiment.

Next she got pregnant, and the same crew plotted another femme fiesta—a *baby* shower.

Wait a minute . . . didn't *you* get her pregnant? Aren't *you* going to be a *full* partner in raising that kid? Where the hell is *your* party?

Have your posse throw you a proper bash for a man with fire in his loins . . . make it a *THUNDERSTORM!*

What venue? Anywhere the women aren't. A boat. RV. The Elks

lodge. Duck blind, deer stand, the beer and shot joint 'round the corner. It matters not, but goddamit this kid will be the biggest accomplishment in your life. *Your kid* is coming . . . what better reason to celebrate?!

Don't invite any business associates. No stiffs! This is strictly for your pals . . . you want only vibes of genuine fellowship. Make sure to include a dad or two and *do not* neglect the old-timers. It's amazing what graybeards know.

If there are to be gifts, make it understood these gifts should enhance your standing as a MACK DADDY. Your wife's baby shower will net all the baby crap you need. The *THUNDER-STORM* is about fortifying your status as the stellar guy you are, ensuring the best possible dad for your kid.

THUNDERSTORM gifts are MACK DADDY fitting. Do you play guitar? How about a set of baby bongos so your kid can jam with you. Fisherman? A kiddie rod and reel. Archer? Baby bow and suction-cup arrows. How about a Three-Stooges library on DVD?

My father was a pretty good carpenter. I *still* recall the smell and feel of a tool belt he gave me with working pliers, hammer and so forth, all downsized for a four-year-old's hands. "We" built a soapbox racer together. And the memory is beyond beautiful. Today, I wouldn't give a nickel for my first real automobile. But I'd pay *anything* for that soapbox car.

Gizmos aside, the real gifts of a *THUNDERSTORM* are the good wishes and approbation of your pals. It's an opportunity to talk with guys that may know more than you do . . . to align yourself with a group that can help you raise a better kid.

Every year, millions of guys blow *billions* on Superbowl parties. If your team wins . . . the players and owners get rings and big bonuses. What do *you* get?

Jack shit.

Every year, in the United States alone, 4.2 million guys become dads. Isn't it time to re-allocate some of that Superbowl $$ to a

THUNDERSTORM? You are going be a *father*—which in the scheme of your life, puts the Superbowl in the toilet bowl.

Make sure you can really rage at the party. If you enjoy swearing, do it—in a few months, your domestic vocabulary will have to echo Mr. Rogers.

Get tanked and howl at the moon. Climb a tree and *hang* a moon. Rent a limo and moon the moon thru the moon roof.

In cultures throughout history fatherhood was hailed as the ultimate rite of passage, as it damn well should be. But modern Western society has slammed the door in Daddy's face. They've hijacked parenting and made it gynocentric. That shit is *over*, my bros. We're back.

The *THUNDERSTORM*. It's the new tradition. Like the Olympic torch, keep it lit and carry it proudly through eternity.

Chapter 2

The Nursery

One mind cannot hold two thoughts simultaneously. This is a blessing. Getting busy will hold fear at bay while building your confidence. It's never too soon to start on the nursery.

When your no-account brother-in-law comes for a visit, you buy him a case of Milwaukee's Best and throw some clean sheets on the spare bed, right? Well, your *child* will be dropping by for about oh, 18–22 years or so . . . doesn't he or she rate some special space? Whether an entire wing of your Biltmore-esque manse or just a corner of your apartment bedroom, it matters not—it's the effort that counts.

Do you know the sex of the child? If it's a boy, *take over!* This is your chance to finally impose your taste (she may have other words for it) in service to your coming scion. . . . Pick a theme and go wild. There are tens of thousands of wallpapers, one of which is sure to reflect you and your son's interests. Flintlocks and cutlasses? Formula Ones and checkered flags? Peterbilts and Kenworths? Go for it.

If it's a girl, you'll want to defer to the missus. Pink and frills and lambs and bunnies are fine.

A newborn's focal range is around 8 to 14 inches. Anything outside of that will be a blur. At about a year a baby's vision reaches full power, so the whole decor thing is about you anyway.

Crap You Need

Say "nursery" and most people think "crib" first. Wrong. The most important thing to have is a *changing table*. They make dozens. Some are good. Many are crap.

Insist that function supersede form. Get one that is sturdy. (Imagine yourself flailing on some shaking, swaying, rickety junk while a strange giant tries to wipe your ass.) The only fear we are born with is the fear of falling, and though your baby won't appreciate gilt filigree, rococo accents, or wicker diaper compartments, he will feel a lot more secure on something solid.

The top shelf must have *four* rails high enough to prevent a roll-off (yes, there will be times when you'll walk away from baby on that table) and a concave, washable vinyl pad. Get a changing table with wheels—they can be heavy and you may want to move it around the house.

There should be one big top drawer into which go items I'll mention later.

Under that, several *open* shelves. Screw the appearance—when shit flies—and believe me, it *will* fly, you won't want to be fumbling with tricky latches, knobs, bolts or drawers—you'll want *instant* access to diapers, wipes and the like. Think shit balls rolling around like marbles. Think green rivers of sludgy diarrhea. Think aerosol projected puke and spit-up, spilled formula, and puddles of pee pee. Let these images guide you away from cutesy white wicker changing tables (imagine yourself with toothpicks and Q-tips trying to clean caked shit out of that wicker) or ones with duvets, rick-rack or any tricky, unnecessary design elements.

One that can hold a bison and be cleaned with a fire hose is about right.

Where to buy? Those smaller, baby specialty shops with the

warm halogen lights and Armani-clad salesgirls usually have high prices. Babies "R" Us has a nice selection and reasonable tariffs. TIP: push or bribe the sales clerk to let you have the floor model. They can be a bitch to assemble and you don't need any extra work right now.

When you get it home, clamp a low-wattage bulb to it (I used an old, amber darkroom safelight). This way, you can see enough to change a diaper at 3 a.m., and you don't have to switch on a room light—thoroughly waking the baby, a sibling, and you.

You don't need a crib—yet. You don't even need a bassinet. An infant will sleep just as soundly on soft blankets in a corner. Or one couch cushion, properly blanketed. But a bassinet *is* cheap, easy to assemble, can be wheeled into any room, and will serve as fine kip for two or three months. Get one that will rock a bit and has wheel locks.

Remember that top drawer in the changing table? Here are seven things you need in there.

1. A good *digital thermometer*. It'll cost around 50 bucks, but it's worth it. Get one that gives you the option of determining temperature via mouth or under the armpit. Some also work rectally or in the ear. (But what kid likes that?)

2. A *snot-sucker* (clinical name: nasal aspirator/suction bulb). Try to cadge a few from the nurses at the hospital. The ones they have are far better than you'll find in a store.

   Babies get colds and their noses fill with mucus, just like yours. Problem is, they don't know they're supposed to blow out all that ropey green goo. You have to remove it for them. If it's crunchy up there, they make a saline spray to soften things up. (Infants can't *pick* their honkers, either.)

   I got my daughter accustomed to the thing long before it was necessary, so when she finally got a cold, she wasn't afraid of it. When I'd change her diaper, I'd squeeze it in her face. This made her laugh like hell.

3. You'll forget about 90 percent of that infant CPR course within

a week. But they usually give you a handy little *CPR manual* to take home. This drawer is a good place for it.

4. *Infant Tylenol, Infant Motrin, and cough syrup.* Sometimes kids throw a fever in a matter of seconds. Left unchecked, a high temperature can cause a febrile seizure, or worse, brain damage. Keep this stuff on hand!

5. *Rubbing alcohol and cotton balls.* Good for sterilizing anything— thermometer tips, the changing pad. If baby gets a fever, sponge her down with rubbing alcohol to help reduce temperature.

6. *Desitin or A&D ointment.* Baby butts can get raw. Some type of ointment may be needed to soothe skin. These two are pretty good.

Cribs. You can pay a load (thousands) for them. If that's the budget, have at it. Even so, as with changing tables, higher price doesn't necessarily mean a better product.

First, that crib had better fit you and your home as well as the baby.

Decide where the crib will be most of the time. In the middle of a room? You'll want one with *two* sliding side rails. Against a wall? One sliding rail will do the job.

Grab a tape measure. Check the width of the doorway to the room where you intend to place the crib. I neglected this detail and assembled the crib in a room with a doorway narrower than the crib. Not smart!

Armed with this doorway measurement, commence shopping.

Primary consideration: operation of the sides. That side will be raised and lowered *thousands* of times. Get one that unlocks with a foot-bar—remember, both hands will be full with a baby when you approach the crib. The rails should be shiny chrome and dampened above and below by coil springs. The assembly should be sturdy metal (avoid plastic components at moving or stress points). That crib side should unlock and move up and down—effortlessly and *noiselessly*. The last thing you want is a tussle with a crib, or baby—waking rails that squeal like a fork on a chalkboard. The top of the side should have plastic on it (most do) for teethers.

If you shop around, you can score one that's pretty good for a couple of hundred bucks or so. Try second-hand and thrift shops, too. Just check it thoroughly and give it a good disinfecting.

Next, you'll need a crib mattress. A seven-pound person does *not* need independent coil springs or three-way comfort zones. A plain, firm, foam mattress, covered in pee pee–proof vinyl will work perfectly and give your baby all the comfort and support it needs.

You can accessorize a crib like a low-rider's Coupe de Ville. Mobiles, busy boxes, white noise and womb sound machines, rocking devices, whatever. Get a bumper that ties to inside of the bars in case your kid's a head banger. These come in all kinds of designs—Darth Vader, Olsen Twins, Popeye and Bluto, and so forth.

If you dig mobility or your quarters are really cramped, there's an engineering marvel that's an excellent alternative to a crib. It's called a Pack 'n Play (manufacturer is Graco) and it's a sturdy crib/playpen that folds up and fits under a bed or in the trunk of a car. The only two drawbacks are it's low-slung, so you need to bend low to grab your baby, and there's no sliding side rail for easy access. But they're well made and great for road trips or when you want to hang with friends and need a mobile, secure kip for the baby.

Wipe warmer. In the course of your kid's infancy, you will go through thousands and thousands of baby wipes. Some smart guy came up with cute little electric cozies for them, usually in the shape of cuddly animals. It might seem like a luxury, but some babies *will* sleep through a diaper change, so why awaken them with an icy wet wipe on the butt?

Diaper pail/Genie. You'll go through thousands of diapers, whether disposable or cloth. You won't always have time to run out to the garbage or laundry, so why not consolidate the trips and stash the trash close by? They make a thing called a Diaper Genie that is essentially a long, narrow trash bag in a plastic can that will hold a hell of a lot of crappy diapers. It's fairly airtight, but don't push your luck—empty it daily. Or, the old-fashioned white porcelain–coated diaper pail has retro appeal and works fine—as long as the lid fits *tight*.

Crap You Don't Need

This section could fill several volumes. Here's the short list of junk marketed to the well intentioned, the unwitting, and the stupid.

Padded doorknob covers—If your newborn is 46 inches tall and walking around drunk, these might be necessary.

Infant kneepads—Must-haves if your baby plays goalie for the Kings or lays ceramic tile for a living.

Corner cushions—These goofy items are shown protecting the corners of coffee tables, armoires, end tables, etc. If you're that paranoid, dress the kid in Nomex long johns, Kevlar full body armor, and a SNELL/DOT certified crash helmet.

DVD/VCR guard—This item may have some merit, as my daughter did once shove a few CDs into the VCR. Of course, had I left the cabinet doors closed, no problem.

8-Piece grooming set—Eyebrow tweezers, hairbrush, and cuticle sticks, for a seven-pound bald person?

Pacifier thermometer with musical fever indicator—When it hits 103, does it play the Peggy Lee standard?

Tidy Tucks—Keep baby's shirt tucked in. Very important, especially when baby's giving the Merger and Acquisition presentation at 3 p.m. sharp. Better get some double-stick tape for her Baume & Mercier, too.

Sleep Soundly sleep positioner including *Sounds of the Womb* CD—Because it's never too soon to start regressing.

Tooth Fairy thingee—Don't stash a loose tooth under the pillow. Slip it into a felt corporate icon that offers the ultimate incisor storage convenience—it has both a tooth pocket and a gift pocket! Commercializes the most basic and ancient childhood myth.

Oven locks—You never know when your infant will mistake the Magic Chef for a tanning booth, grab a step stool, and climb in, trying to rid himself of his unsightly pallor. Better safe than sorry!

Temperature Control

What's a critical factor in a good night's sleep? The temperature. It has to be j-u-u-u-st right. For you, a snap. But baby can't tell you his preferences. My daughter used to roll around like a pinball, rendering futile any attempt to keep her covered. Our home has a one-zone heat system, so what to do?

Answer: a hot oil radiator, around $60. You can get them at Home Depot, Lowe's, and those big-chain drug stores. These things are great. Looks like an old-fashioned cast-iron, hot-water radiator. But it's filled with oil. You plug it in, and in about five minutes it throws heat like a pot-bellied stove. It smells a little the first time you use it, but after that, it emits no sound, light, or odor. The perfect space heater for baby's area.

Avoid heaters with any type of gas power or electric/quartz ones with hot wires. They're okay on construction sites—not in your kid's room.

When it's summer and stifling, a window air conditioner will get the job done. Besides energy efficiency, they rate them on noise— something to consider if the baby's a light sleeper.

Light Control

How do you give the finest home the depressing look and feel of a prison camp? Fluorescent lighting.

An old newspaper story claimed fluorescents emit an ultrasonic squeal that, over time, will drive you nuts. Could be true. If not, this *is* a stone fact: they throw the harshest, ugliest, most unflattering light in the entire visible spectrum. They don't belong in your kitchen or bathroom, and certainly not in the baby's room.

In the nursery, you want two (incandescent, tungsten—ordinary soft white) lights, maybe three. First, a wall or ceiling fixture that will light up the entire room. Next, a lamp with a soft shade. Key word: *dimmers*. Babies tend to like everything gradual, and lights are no different. To go from bright light to total darkness, or vice versa, is jarring and unpleasant. Dimmers really facilitate naps and bedtime. You can buy them in any configuration—as wall switches or sliders on an extension cord. When you put the baby down for a nap and check on it, dim the lights with each successive visit. Cheap, effective, and they make a difference.

If you like, there are all kinds of variations of lightbulbs—soft pink, peach, and other tints. Some come with opaque tops so they don't throw scary shadows on the ceiling. An outfit called Varilux makes bulbs that duplicate the wavelength of sunlight. Expensive, but nice.

Many people put a night light in the nursery. Use this only if necessary. Most kids don't need a night light until some adult spooks them about the dark. MACK DADDIES don't create fear in their kids, they remove it.

On the windows, again, function trumps form. Have all the lace or bamboo or alabaster vellum window treatments you want, but they had better be accompanied by something that's *opaque*. The more that kid sleeps, the more you will, too. Get wooden shutters, blackout shades, or drapes. These may be the most important weapon in your baby sleep arsenal. Many a night, that kid will be up for a variety of reasons only to fall into a deep sleep before dawn. Don't let sunlight screw things up. Get those blackout shades!

Sound Control

Walk into the nursery-to-be and clap your hands. If it echoes like a blimp hangar, you have work to do. Sure, those hardwood or tile floors are attractive and low maintenance. And from an acoustic perspective, they're just right—for Michael Flatley. When that baby cries it will be loud enough to crack the Mikasa. Factor in reverberations caused by bare floors, walls, and ceilings and you'll be boning up on American Sign Language.

Get a big area rug.

If you've always dreamed of hanging an acoustic tile ceiling, now's the time to live that fantasy.

Is your nursery motif Teamster Cocktail Lounge? Go ahead— spray the ceilings with that cottage cheese crap—they may even still make it in my favorite shade and texture—Hematoma Sparkle.

If you've been thinking about re-doing the windows with double panes, start with this room first. Think ahead. It may be quiet now, but once your baby comes, that moron next door will decide to convert his garage to a dog kennel, raise prize roosters, or tune Harleys in his driveway, which will keep your kid—and you— awake.

Do anything to deaden sound. Oil the door hinges. Wax the squeaky runners on the chest of drawers. Hang that velvet Elvis right between the velour matador and those poker-playing dogs. If it absorbs sound, it's beautiful.

If you work from home, or frequently conduct business from home, nursery acoustics are doubly important to you. Imagine yourself on the phone, trying to finesse the Framazoid account while your baby wails in the background. This will not add to your stature as a wheeler-dealer.

MACK DADDY Rides

If you're Amish, a Zuni cliff dweller, or dig the stench, discomfort, and danger of public transportation, skip this section. But if horsepower, torque, and compression ratios quicken your pulse, read on.

Long ago, when families grew to more than two or three kids, people traded their Bugs, Corvairs, and Darts for *station wagons.*

Wagons held eight or nine people pretty comfortably. They could tow an Airstream or Chris-Craft. They held luggage, beach balls, skis, camping gear—all kinds of crap. Some had cool, rear-facing jump seats where kids could make faces at or flip the bird to the cars behind.

Their name was derived from perfectly coiffed Donna Reed mommies driving from their perfect suburban homes to the train *station* to pick up pipe-smoking, fedora-wearing Hugh Beaumont/Carl Betz dads. But even then, they held a certain stigma that manufacturers tried to camouflage with jaunty or landed-gentry model names. Ford Country Squire. Pontiac Safari. Chevy Nomad (the two-door '57 is a coveted classic) Chrysler Town & Country. Buick Sportswagon. Olds Vista Cruiser (with groovy raised roof and curved glass corner panels). *Hey kids! An observation deck!*

Some were pretty cool rigs. During the '60s James Bond craze, Dean Martin played a soused secret agent in a flick (first of a series of four) called *The Silencers.* He drove a big-ass '66 Mercury Colony Park wagon. It had a backseat bar replete with crystal decanters. And, at the touch of a button, it deployed an inflatable jumbo Sultan's tent, tricked out for a roadside orgy.

Alas, they were still *station wagons.* Todd Styles and Buzz Murdock did not set off down *Route 66* in search of hot chicks and adventure in a Country Squire.

Then came the '80s and minivans. Dreamed up by Lee Iacocca

(the same smoothy who convinced America that the Mustang was a *sports* car) the minivan was the official ride of Soccer Moms.

Then came the '90s and the SUV. (Not really. The Ford Bronco, Jeep Wagoneer, Chevy Suburban were around long before the '90s). But everybody *knows* SUVs are minivans in disguise. And a minivan is just a station wagon with high sides. And high sides mean crummy aerodynamics, lousy handling, and a tendency to roll over.

Funny how many newer (Chrysler, Lexus, Subaru, Ford) "SUVs" have lower profiles and look a hell of a lot like . . . *station wagons!* Everything old is new again.

So, what will we drive?

The Hayabusa and the 575 GTC are a little shy on cargo space and cupholders. Let's look at some alternatives.

Minivans . . . for Minimen?

Minivans are not cool. They never will be. Even *Get Shorty* couldn't make them cool. They look and drive like a refrigerator. So why hasn't Detroit yet added egg shelves, a butter door, ice-maker, and a salad crisper? Any day now.

MACK DADDY Automotive mythbuster: Until you have three or more kids, why do you need a minivan?

With two adults and two or three kids, who needs seating for nine and all that vertical sprawl? A four-door sedan will handle better, get better mileage, be safer and far cooler. Minivan cargo space, unless you start removing or folding seats, is usually a miniscule area between the rearmost seat and the rear door. Which, unlike a nice opaque trunk, leaves your precious stuff visible to thieves.

Even soccer moms don't want to be seen in them. If you already own one, or have three or more kids and need one, okay . . . but *please,* no bumper stickers of any kind, especially for your alma mater. A MACK DADDY's cool demeanor trumpets his credentials, not some pathetic decal. Yecch! If you've ever owned (or have considered owning) a *My Child Is an Honor Student at Meconium Academy* bumper sticker . . . well, we won't even go there.

Here's another great reason not to drive all that seating room. Once your toddler starts nursery school, you'll be amazed at all the new best friends your wife and you will collect. All this fellowship will generate group activities—beach trips, picnics, and so on. If you have the capacity, you'll be selected for chauffer duties. If one screaming toddler gives you a migraine, imagine the pain you're in for with several. With a four-door sedan, you can leave the driving to the other guy.

S.U.V. = T.N.M.V. (The New Minivan)
You ain't foolin' *nobody*.

They get rotten mileage. They're expensive to insure. They roll over. They are cliché. You can do better.

How did millions of families travel billions of road miles in Impalas, Le Sabres, Catalinas, Fleetwoods, and Eight-eights without one single cupholder, GPS, or flat-screen TV?

If you've scored a nice sedan—5 or 7 series BMW, Benz, Lexus, or Infiniti Q, why screw around with ersatz trucks?

Hate investing all that jing in a depreciating asset? Here are some more alternatives.

For decades, those FoMoCo guys have cranked out millions upon millions of cars that are just perfect for MACK DADDIES. Whether called Crown Victoria, Mercury Grand Marquis, or Lincoln Town Cars, they're all the *same* car. They have pretty much identical drive trains—a ballsy V-8, silky automatic transmission, and *rear*-wheel drive. (What's good about that? Nearly every race and performance car is RWD. And other manufacturers are getting back to RWD—certain models of

Infiniti, Lexus, even Cadillac. Why? With more even weight distribution, they handle better—period.)

Why do cops, Mafia Dons, limo and cab companies love the FoMoCo barges? Because fleet managers know that with minimal maintenance, they'll go 300,000 miles or *more*. They'll hold six adults. Their deep-well trunks will engulf a Mini Cooper. They're quiet, stable, crash-worthy, quick, and at highway speeds will average as much as 23 or 24 mpg. You can buy them basic for less than a bland Accord or dress them up like Bourbon Street tarts and spend a lot more—it's your choice. Regardless, you get a hell of a ride and salvation from minivan and SUV conformity.

Those crafty cats at Toyota have been banging out their own Crown Victoria for many years. (In fact, in Japan they used to market a car called the Crown.) The Camry is probably the best value in imported cars. Although they won't seat six, they will hold five pretty comfortably. They handle like bandits, are quiet, sturdy, and will cruise at 80 like they're standing still. And they go forever.

There's a lot to be said for the Chrysler 300, with its screaming Hemi and boulevardier styling—it will hold all your crap, run like a cheetah, and redeem you from suburban compliance. Thinking of moonlighting as a NASCAR driver? Consider the Mopar madmen's 6.1 liter, 425 horsepower Dodge Charger. With a functional hood scoop, front fascia, and rear spoiler, you'll never be mistaken for a soccer mom.

There are a bunch of four-door sedans out there that can be really well equipped, are fun to drive, and utilitarian. If you're buying used, they make a great choice—because odds are, the previous owner was an AARP member and only drove it to and from bingo. Invest a few bucks in www.carfax.com.

If you're buying new, facing the showroom grip 'n' grin cobras is another book entirely. But here are a few quick tips to keep in mind before entering that arena.

- Timing—of the year *and* month—is crucial. Best time of year, late summer/early fall when dealers have to empty their lots for fresh metal.

- If you need the car *now,* try to wait until the end of the month. They have sales quotas to meet and the end of the month is when they get desperate. Don't let them waste your time. They get paid to hang around the showroom all day—you don't. The longer they can keep you hanging with *let me check with my manager,* the more time you've invested and less likely you are to walk. If they can't give you a written price on a car within 15 minutes, leave.

- Here's a great tactic that really cuts the bullshit. Around the 29th or 30th of the month, send a few dealers a fax listing the car, options, and price or lease payment you want. Tell them if they can meet your criteria, you will buy *today.* Smart ones respond. Saves you legwork and negotiating hassles.

Purge the Garage/Basement/Attic Now

They call space "the final frontier." True enough, but it's also the reason for nearly all of the fights, wars, and battles in the history of mankind. Everybody from Genghis to Hitler, Stalin and Saddam has wanted more and been willing to kill for it.

Why do you bust your ass working so hard? Isn't it really so you can get out of that crummy cramped pad and into digs with more room, away from those asshole neighbors and their goddamn boom boxes, yappy mutts, leaf blowers, and accordions? Why do people prefer limos to buses and subways? Space man, space . . . you can never get enough of it.

Guess who's gonna annex more of your square footage than a dictator? Your baby. There will be a bassinet, a crib (with blankies, sheets, and pillows for each) bouncy chairs, goofy animal-themed floor pads with crap strung overhead they can stare at, sink tubs, bathtub chairs, kiddie potties, kiddie toilet seats, stacks of diapers, wipes, diaper pails and genies, car seats, kiddie corrals, Pack 'n Plays (a crib/corral to go) toys, strollers, jogging strollers—in short, one kid can accrue more crap in a few months than a Salvation Army semi. Where are you going to stash all that stuff?

Well, everywhere. And that stuff is expensive. If you're planning on having more than one kid, you'll have to *store* all that shit. Checked the local DIY warehouse lately? Those larcenous bums are getting $100 a month for a 5-by-5 bin. That will barely hold one crib.

Smart MACK DADDIES start purging storage space before the baby's born. Hit the attic, basement, and garage and start tossing crap now. You cannot believe how fast it piles up.

Go Splurge Now on a High-End Camera

Guys love gadgets—especially MACK DADDIES. We dig tricky gizmos. It's in our nature.

If you got a yen for a new camera, now's the time. Of course, digital is the way to go. Just a few years ago, they were novelties that serious photographers wouldn't allow in the studio. Now, film cameras are obsolete.

Everybody wants megapixels. Is more better? Yeah, but three or four is all you really need, unless you're planning on making mural-sized prints.

The point-and-shoots with the telephoto lenses are pretty good. And since this is all about your kid, odds are *smaller is better*. If you can jam it in a shirt pocket, you'll use it a lot more than the digital SLR that needs a carrying case and neck strap.

Digital zooms are meaningless bullshit—the optical power is what counts. The minimum is 3x; 10x is great, but all that glass is going to make it bigger and heavier. One of the world's greatest photographers once said, "The best zoom lens is your legs." Not only is a 10x lens heavier, you'll need the stability of an Easter Island Moai to hold it steady at that focal length.

Two *very* important factors to consider that they won't mention on the side of the box are: the length of time it takes for it to boot up from the moment you turn it on, and the lag time between when you press the shutter release and the image is made. Naturally, in both cases, shorter is better, but check it out before you buy. (Canon and Nikon's high-end cameras have pretty much eliminated boot-up and shutter lag and offer blistering burst rates, for you action freaks.)

Many of the smaller digi-cams lack an optical viewfinder. This is a *serious* flaw. On a sunny day, an LCD viewfinder is worthless. Make sure it has an optical viewfinder.

Is it ergonomic? Can you operate it comfortably with one hand? (You should be able to.) Is that optical viewfinder bright and clear and free of distortion? Can you squeeze the shutter release and zoom in and out with the camera pressed to your face?

They'll all give you a choice of size of memory card. A 16-megabyte chip may only store 30 or so images. Go for at least a 256k or 512. On a 5-megapixel camera, using fairly high-resolution settings, you can pack away around 420 images on a 512k memory card—that's good enough for a very well-documented vacation. And of course, you can delete the ones you don't like at any time.

Now, here's where it gets tricky, and you'll appreciate the importance of a quick boot-up and minimal shutter lag—in the delivery room.

Anything can happen at any time. Your wife can be pushing for hours and hours, but once that baby "crowns" as they say in the biz, he can pop out like a champagne cork. If you want those once-in-a-lifetime, first-breath pictures of your baby, you better be on Defcon-1 high alert. Make sure the camera is on and booted up. Have the batteries well charged. Snap that baby as it debuts. See that blurriness in the viewfinder? It's your tears, tough guy.

This is the most beautiful sight you will ever see, and if it doesn't put a throb in your heart and a lump in your throat, nothing will.

Risky Regimens for Mommas to Be

In the Buns-of-Steel American zeitgeist, most women want six-pack abs and an ass you can crack eggs on. These are admirable traits, but maybe not while she's cooking a baby.

My wife, after learning she was pregnant, kept swimming her laps and working that Stairmaster. Then one day, at around the five-month mark, we went for a routine visit to the ultrasound man.

He lowered the lights. He flicked on the gizmo, squirted the goop, and started playing Hot Wheels on her belly with that sonar wand thing. Usually, this guy was very chatty, gabbing throughout the procedure. But this time, his chitchat ceased and silence prevailed. The silence was, as they say, deafening. Irene's hand gripped mine so tightly, I heard bones crack.

When he finally spoke, he told us there was a problem with the fetus's heart. Blood was leaking from chamber to chamber. What could cause such a thing? He ticked off a list. When he said the words "Down syndrome," I started to pray. Then he asked Irene how physically active she was. She described her exercise regimen. He told her to knock it off and go to complete bed rest for three weeks, while trying to stay on her left side. After that, it was four hours a day bed rest for the remainder of her pregnancy.

Irene hit the couch. She broke my balls relentlessly, in a specially formulated voice that sounded like some 95-year-old, demanding, petulant bag. *Young man, would you bring me some water puh-leeze? With ice, puh-leeze?* I'd bring the water. *Would you crush the ice, puh-lease, young man?* It was pretty funny, and we laughed a lot. But beneath it all ran an undercurrent of fear and anxiety.

Finally came the time to return to the chatty ultrasound guy and miracles of miracles, that baby's heart valve had healed. The doctor explained what happened, in terms I think I understood.

That fetus needs a steady and heavy flow of nutrition from Mommy. When Mom plays decathlon competitor, what should be going to that baby is diverted to Mom's heart, lungs, and muscles. Baby loses. There are stats that back up this theory—heavy workout chicks often produce lower-birth-weight babies.

It makes sense. Most mammals slow down in pregnancy. Since the dawn of time, pregnancy was considered a delicate condition. Women were expected to take it easy and do nothing strenuous. Now, uber-chix feel some compulsion to remain shredded even in pregnancy. It's nutty.

How often in life do you get a nine-month free pass for self-indulgence and indolence? Sounds like a pretty good deal. Mommy can always go back to her fitness model regimen after the baby. But while she's cooking it, she should probably take it easy.

Not that she has to live the life of veal. There are loads of pregnant-mom yoga classes. Floating around in a pool and a leisurely lap or two is okay, too. But the ten-mile hikes, power-lifts and Tae Bo are better left to times after the baby is born.

Chapter 3

The Name Game

This is where MACK DADDIES *must* exert influence—especially if the child is male. Girls get some slack for frilly, goofy handles. Boys don't. Since your wife doesn't know what it's like to have a schoolyard full of boys chanting *farty Marty* at her, she may not understand.

Kids can be nasty. In a group they can turn lethal. Your son's name must be *bulletproof*. John, Michael, David, Edward, William, James, Mark—these classic names are Kevlar. There's just no way to distort, bastardize, or most important, feminize them.

Three names *never* to give your son:

1. Dick

2. Jesus

3. Adolph

Avoid the overly tough or heroic—Zeus, Apollo, Genghis, Hercules, Sinbad, Beowulf, Spike, Adonis, Jupiter, Samson, Hannibal—unless your kid bursts from the womb with the physique of the Incredible Hulk, he may have some difficulty living up to these names.

Ditto Strength, Justice, Truth, Virtue, Fortitude, Courage, Miracle.

Stay away from characters from literature and mythology. Sure, Aladdin's a cool name. But it's also a thermos. Homer will become Homo, guaranteed. Ulysses will be "you pussy."

Thinking of naming your kid after a living celebrity? Think Orenthal James Simpson. Kobe Bryant. Corey Feldman.

People think it's cool to tag their kid with some family surname. Beware. How many little "Jacksons" take heat thanks to the King of Pop's peccadilloes? You never know what cretin with your distinguished family name might be tomorrow's psycho killer. Who would name a kid Manson, Dahmer, or Gacy?

Androgynous names—for a boy? Not good. Lindsey, Ashley, Brook, Lynne, Taylor are cute—for girls.

Elemental/nature names—Earth, Wind, Fire, Sea, Sunshine, Eagle, Oak, Jaguar, Rainbow, Tropic of Cancer, Horse Latitudes, Sargasso, Van Allen Belt, Manatee, Blowfish—nah.

Trendy TV and movie character names are risky, too. What's hip today is clichéd tomorrow. You can pretty much peg a kid's age by the following trendoid monikers:

Dylan, Brandon: 1990—*Beverly Hills 90210*

Tristan: 1994—*Legends of the Fall*

Neo, Morpheus, Trinity: 1999—*The Matrix*

Chad: 2000—The contentious presidential election

Three names NEVER to give your daughter:

1. Bertha

2. Ethel

3. Irma

Why? They just *sound* awful. Like tuba notes.

Locations—use caution. There's **Reno, Dallas, Troy, Dakota**. But as with celebs, it's risky. Think Columbine. Chernobyl. Auschwitz.

Celebrities think they have a license to saddle their kids with kooky handles. Sean Penn—*Hopper*. David Bowie—*Zowie* (now Joey). Bruce Willis—*Rumor, Scout,* and *Tallulah*. David Beckham and Posh Spice—*Brooklyn, Romeo*. Rob Morrow named his daughter *Tu. Tu-Morrow*. Jason Lee and Beth Riesgraf—*Pilot Inspektor*. Shannyn Sossamon and Dallas Clayton—*Audio Science*. Nicholas Cage named his kid *Kal-El*—Superman's Krytptonian name.

Does a tricky spelling make a kid's name more original, or give him ownership of it? Unlikely. He'll spend a lifetime repeating it for teachers, receptionists, coworkers, and bosses. Why complicate his life? Is there really a difference between Jennifer and Jenifyr? Why make a Daniel into Danyal? They'll only wind up calling him Denial.

Watch the initials! Alan Steven Simmons is a perfectly good name that guarantees your son will be called **A.S.S.** Ponder the monogram *before* you christen.

Bob Evans, Hollywood legend and former Garmento, referenced a bit of wisdom that's been floating around NYC's fashion district forever. "If you wear a new shirt and somebody says 'Hey, nice shirt,' great. If it happens again, throw it away—the shirt is wearing *you*." The same reasoning applies to names.

If you tag your kid with some heinous handle and subsequently realize the error, change his name. Some very famous folks were thusly saved by name changes:

• Genghis Kahn: His birth name—*Temujin*—would have consigned him to lackey status for all of his days. Genghis Kahn (True Leader) is a lot cooler, no?

• Sitting Bull: Originally named *Slow*. (*Hey everybody, Slow is coming, and he looks pissed! Walk! Walk for your lives!*)

- Crazy Horse: Birth name—*Curly*. Luckily his dad came to his senses.

If you don't change your kid's goofy name to something better, he may decide to do so himself. The results can be catastrophic. These self-named guys are some of the biggest assholes the world has ever known.

- Joe Stalin: Birth name—Loseb Dzhugashvili. Renamed himself Man of Steel and killed 20 million to live up to the moniker.

- Adlof Hitler: His old man's actual name was Schicklgruber. *Heil Schicklgruber?*

- Pol Pot: Birth name, Saloth Sar (aka "brother number one"). He killed about 3 million brothers.

A kid's name is a critical choice of his life—in which he has zero say. Be kind. Be smart. Do *not* indulge yourself. The name is about him or her, not Mom and Dad's ego, pedigree, cleverness, or serendipitous, devil-may-care attitude. Hanging an oddball name on a child *will* cause problems.

If, at adulthood, your Joe decides he'd rather be called Mushroom Cloud, Bilge Rat, or Melissa, that's his choice.

Birthing Classes: The Agony and . . . the Agony

For a first birth, you can't say no and still be a MACK DADDY. But for subsequent births, if somebody mentions *birthing class*, just scream NOOOOOOOOOOOOOO!

Birthing classes are kind of like an encounter group for kooks. You'll get more information than you need or want. Hours of gory, amateur-porn-caliber films of emergency-room mayhem. And why is this? Birthing classes are not designed for MACK DADDIES and their exemplary wives. They are for the masses. And everything about them feels, sounds, and smells like a public clinic.

The two-hour sessions are spread over six weeks. Some are offered as full-day or weekend marathon sessions. They go over every detail of childbirth, from breathing to epidurals to what can go oh-so-wrong. What they do is make it all stultifyingly dull and puff it up to fill time. The volume of *necessary* info could be imparted in 15 minutes.

If you're married to some Birkenstock chick who wants "natural" childbirth at home with a midwife—she better have the pain threshold of a lobotomized ox. In this case, pay careful attention and take notes. You'll need every bit of info to help handle the situation at home.

But if she's going the more conventional route, once you get her to the hospital, they do pretty much everything and you're just there to hold her hand and take verbal abuse—which she will heap on you with vitriol until she ends her "I don't want an epidural" charade. This is the femme equivalent of the macho dare. Some chicks actually get competitive about this lunacy. Why, we'll never know. Do they ever, even for an instant try to gut out a root canal sans anesthetic? No way. So what's up with the Earth-Mother/Buffalo Wallow Woman routine? Though most wimp out (and who can blame them?) sometimes they'll still try to out-do one another with the "Oh yeah? Well I was in labor *two* hours before I got *my* epidural!" Well hoo-ray for you, baby!

So, if she wants to go to labor classes, go along, but bring an MP3 player or something to read.

What to Do When She Goes into Labor

Races to the hospital make great scenes in movies. In reality, they are quite rare. The average amount of time women spend in labor is 12 hours. So what's the rush? Of course, sometimes labor can be a lot shorter, but 12 hours should negate any need for haste.

Here's the drill. When she starts feeling contractions, they might be 20 or 30 minutes apart. She usually feels stomach cramps that get more intense. Sometimes they feel like back pain. Unless the hospital is very far away, you've got enough time to do some things—and you'll wish you had if you don't.

- Take a shower. You might be at that hospital a long time.

- Double-check both your bags for all the stuff you need.

- Have something to eat at home.

- She'll call the doctor. He'll ask how far apart the contractions are, and based on that, decide whether she should head for the hospital.

- Before you leave the house, have a look around. When you return, God willing, you'll have a new tenant. And if you like the Zen, uncluttered look of your MACK DADDY domicile, snap a picture, because that's the last time you'll see it that way for at least 18 years.

- If you spend Sundays Lexol-ing your Corinthian leather car seats, you might want to spread a towel on her seat in case her water breaks.

Once you hit the road, take it easy. If her contractions are powerful and close together and she's writhing in pain, she'll make you nervous. But once you get her though the doors of the hospital, they'll quickly get things set. Different hospitals in different parts of the country have their own methods.

With our first child, Irene was put in a triage unit for two hours. When the action started heating up, they moved her to a delivery room.

Prepare yourself for the bizarre. There are some pretty noticeable visual cues that a woman is in labor. Big bloated belly. Doubled over in pain. Grimaces. When Irene was in labor the second time, the admitting nurse asked, "When is the baby due?"

As we exited the elevator to the maternity ward, another nurse looked at my very obviously in labor wife and chirped (without a hint of irony), "So, what brings you in this morning?"

Remember, it may be a first time for both of you, but only a few billion couples have been through this before you. She's hard-wired to do this. It will go fine. Relax.

You Are Not Alone: Some Dadly Digits

There are around 66.5 million dads in America. Surprisingly, fewer than 100,000 are stay-at-home dads.

- 5% of them are over 55
- 11% are under 30
- 21% are raising 3 or more kids under the age of 18

Single fathers comprise 2.3 million.
Of those:

- 42% are divorced
- 38% never married
- 15% are separated
- 5% are widowed
- 10% are raising infants
- 22% are under 30
- 1% are over 65

Fathers who are paying child support number 4.6 million.

Of the men who are required to pay child support, 68 percent do, while only 57 percent of women who are required to pay child support meet their obligation. (Can you say *deadbeat mom*?)

Source: U.S. Census.

Your Hospital Survival Kit

Labor ain't no stroll down Sesame Street. It's one bitch of a marathon. Expect the unexpected. She'll probably have her bag packed with her stuff an hour after she knows she's pregnant. But being a MACK DADDY, you'll be right beside her for the whole ordeal—an ordeal that could take 8, 18, 36 hours . . . or more. And since your bambino will appear when he or she damn well pleases, you dare not split for a short beer at the corner bar. You might miss everything and be in the marital shit-house for eternity.

Be smart—pack your own bag. What to put in it? Food. First time around, I packed two woefully inadequate granola bars. Not only was hunger burning a hole in my belly, my "hungry breath" could have knocked maggots off a cat turd.

My wife was in labor for ten hours—starting at 3 a.m., so I was basically food-less for 18 hours. All they'll let her eat is ice chips, so if you wanna be a Lactating/Rubber Stamp daddy, bring nothing and starve along with her.

A MACK DADDY is most useful when properly fed and hydrated, so bring some serious grub and drink. Wanna be Johnny Romantic? Bring a bottle of boozeless champagne (do *not* give her the real thing—she'll be so full of industrial-strength drugs, you dare not add hooch to it) and a few plastic champagne flutes and pop the cork a few minutes after they get your newborn cleaned up. You'll be a legend in that hospital. Your wife will worship you. The labor nurses will want to do you.

Cell phone. You'll be calling everyone you know . . . why pay the hospital rates?

Bring a novel. Bring a crossword. Bring coloring books. Bring Play-Doh and sculpt busts of the labor crew, making sure to ask their opinions of their likenesses. Bring Rock 'em Sock 'em Robots, make the blue guy your wife and the red one the baby and call the fight in Marv Albert's voice. Bring a flask of Yukon Jack. Bring a camera. Bring a video camera. Maybe the obstetrician is a foxy chick and you can tape the whole process then edit it into a hot and kinky soft-core girl/girl porn short called *Stirrups 'n' Scrubs*. Bring a DVD player and the newest release from Wicked Video. Hold the screen up to the anesthesiologist and say, *Hey Doc, whaddya think of this money shot?* Bring naughty photos of your wife in her CFM shoes, fishnets, garter belt, and half-cups. During a big contraction, think Dennis Hopper in *Blue Velvet* or *Speed*, shove them in her face and tell her you expect her to look this way again *within ten days—two weeks MAX!*

There must be some deep, karmic meaning to childbirth, although I'll be dipped in shit if I can divine it. You *know* how sexy it was putting that baby in her belly . . . why then, is expelling it as erotic as an Al Qaeda beheading?

But seriously, folks, even with the drugs, it's a painful, grueling, and scary experience. You can sit there like some asshole daddy in an asshole TV show and hold her hand and stroke her forehead and tell her to breathe and push and hold on and all that other wimpus, AMA-approved behavior from the birthing class, or you can git yer stubbly face right up in hers and belch, or make faces or do impressions or tell filthy jokes or sing Barnacle Bill or whatever the hell it takes to push her *laugh* button. That's what I did to my wife in the final throes of her second labor. I sang the Popeye song *as* Popeye, described, sotto voce, a threesome between Bluto, Olive Oyl, and my sister-in-law, and when she begged me to shut up, I explained, in African click talk, why I could not.

I am convinced her laughter made that baby shploop outta her like a greased peach.

When our baby appeared, just like with the first, a curious silence fell over the room. No crying, as written-by-childless-clueless TV writers. The baby made no sound. The doc smiled and wiped the blood and goop off her and laid her on my wife's chest and she sighed a sigh as anyone would at the end or the beginning of an endless journey, and my throat lumped and my eyes welled up and I counted ten fingers and toes and thanked Big MACK DADDY for the greatest gift I could ever be given.

Then the baby cried, and everybody laughed.

The beauty of the labor room is that no matter how 21st-century mankind tries to sanitize, civilize, and Martinize the process, it's still totally primordial—a female mammal fulfilling her biological destiny—and therefore, you and especially your wife are licensed to say and do pretty much whatever you want to. The labor nurses and doctors have seen every outlandish behavior imaginable, and, short of spraying the room with a MAC-10, will be unfazed by your comments or antics. So let it all hang out, bro'! It don't get any real-er than this. Perhaps that's another inherent beauty and truth (aren't they one and the same?) of the medical profession. Sick people, dying people, people in pain, people in labor tend to drop all their acts, pretensions, and attitudes. They say and do as they feel, and nobody blames them for their honesty.

Epidurals: This Is Your Wife/ This Is Your Wife on Drugs

The scene is always played out the same way. Expectant mom digs organic foods, herbal remedies, and hemp jogging suits. She's heard about so-and-so who recently gave birth naturally, i.e., sans anesthesia. (Note: so-and-so is never a direct friend—as with most urban legends, she's always a friend of a friend.)

In her ninth month, said friend strolled out into a field of daisies, removed her Birkenstocks, squatted, chanted a Nepalese pain-reduction mantra, and in a matter of minutes, gave birth painlessly—aided only by her friend Windsong, who, after chewing through the umbilical cord, wrapped the infant in stone-washed burlap, held him aloft in praise and thanks to Goddess and named him . . . Shecky.

This apocryphal tale has been circling the globe as long as the "I bought a babe a drink at the airport and woke up in a tub of ice minus a kidney" story. Many women find it appealing, and who wouldn't? Daisies and sunshine beat tile, stainless steel, and fluorescents. A calm, knowing midwife, resembling Pocahontas, beats hell out of Dr. Friedman the Ob/Gyn, who resembles Larry David.

As appealing as this bullshit story is, most women hedge their birthing bets and cherry-pick elements from the fantasy. Seeking the relative security of 21st-century medicine, they go to the hospital, but announce upon arrival they will definitely *not* be needing an epidural. Upon hearing this, the Ob/Gyns must bite holes in their tongues trying to suppress the laughter. Then they run down the hall and place bets with the rest of the floor crew as to what time nature girl will first shriek *GIMMETHEFUCKING DRUGS!*

Unfortunately by then, there may not be an anesthesiologist in the house. They may have to send out for one, and maybe it's his poker night and he's got a $10,000 stack of chips (chump change to these guys—wait'll you see the bill!) in front of him and *I'm gonna play another few hands and nature girl can wait.*

There she lies, huffing and puffing and trying all the pain-reduction techniques from the class, but nothing would reduce that pain like a few dozen CCs of Novocain mainlined into her lower back.

What exactly is an epidural? *Epi* means "surrounding" and *dura* refers to the spine. (Is that how they came up with *EpiLady* razors?) There's this tissue around the spine where the nerve endings disperse and it's that space where they jab her with one big-ass needle full of zoom juice. Then, they connect an IV to it so they can pump more drugs into her as needed.

That's the only time I felt really afraid for my wife. When the Zonk Doctor strolled in pushing a tray with a blue napkin draped over a syringe the size of a Bud Tall Boy, I got queasy. Luckily, these guys know the drill and make sure Mommy never gets to eyeball the spike. But it's damn scary to think of somebody poking around near spinal tissue—visions of Chris Reeve and Stephen Hawking loomed large.

If your wife insists on playing it au naturel, be sure to wear ear plugs and an athletic cup. In the agony of contractions, through eyes clamped shut with blinding pain, they often seek and find the source of all this suffering—your testicles—and try to kick, crush, or rip them from their moorings. Beware.

When they finally cave and request the dose, maintain your distance. Even if Zonk Doc's aim is true, it takes a while for the junk to kick in. Once it does, she's numb from the ass down. Sometimes they miss the "spot" and have to jab again. Look out!

So, MACK DADDY, try to encourage your chick to embrace modern medicine and spare everybody the whole, goofy, counterproductive charade.

What will those other guys do?

- We *know* what Der Fuehrer Daddy's act will be. He'll goose step up to wifey, put on his best Willem Dafoe face, and shriek *take the pain!!*

- Lactating Daddy will grimace and wail along with Mommy— they are just thisclose. When she caves and requests the epidural, Lactating Daddy will ask if he can have one too— 'cause he just wants to *share the experience.*

- Distant Daddy will phone in from the 12th hole and ask the nurse how everything is going. Then he'll have to put her on call-waiting.

To Cut or Not to Cut

You move, yet you are weightless. You hear sounds—children playing, music, traffic—but it's all muted and doesn't disturb your sleep-like state. If you hunger, you are fed—effortlessly. Your every need is immediately fulfilled. Your comfort is complete.

The dream begins to unravel. You feel strange pressures. You are being slowly squeezed and moved downward. This does not feel right. You are scared. Very scared. The pressure on your head is almost unbearable. Sounds are getting louder, Suddenly, BLINDING LIGHT and DEAFENING NOISE. You can't really see, everything is bright and blurry. You feel as if your shoulders are being crushed. It's cold. You are so, so frightened.

You feel comforting warmth and softness and hear a voice, a voice so familiar—a voice that was once was a murmur has clarity. You feel soft hands stroke you, warm lips on your cheek. Your fear subsides.

Suddenly, you are taken from those loving arms and laid on your back on a cold, metal table. Your ankles and wrists are bound. And you scream. You scream in excruciating agony as somebody slashes the end of your tiny penis and rips a piece of flesh from it.

Planning on having your baby son circumcised?

Here are a few points to ponder. How the hell did circumcision begin? According to many historians, it was a way to mark slaves. (Even though you name your kid Rex, his dick says Charley Chattel.) But, history aside, can you think of any other creature whom, upon birth, is surgically altered for no valid reason whatsoever, other than it's a *tradition*?

A few years back, there was a show on National Geographic or somewhere that profiled a little-known South American tribe. These folks take piercing to an extreme the kids on Melrose Avenue haven't dreamed of. They think it's really stylish to pound what resembles the butt end of a billiard cue under the tongue, and through the lower jaw, so it protrudes out of their chins about three or four inches. No doubt this makes eating, shaving, and oral sex a tad complicated, but, *hey, it's a tradition!*

In other regions of the world, from Africa to the Middle East, Australia and New Zealand, people like to mutilate their daughters as well, and perform some 2 million female circumcisions (also called clitoridectomies) or FGM (female genital mutilation). Reasons for this *tradition* include curbing female sexual desire *(that'll keep Tiffany away from that boy at the 7-Eleven!)*, eliminating promiscuity *(the little whore!)*, preserving virginity (if it becomes infected and gangrene sets in, her virginity will *definitely* be preserved), and lastly, that the clitoris is an unattractive, unnecessary thing. *Yecch!*

Ready for the disconnect? While male circumcision is called normal and is legal throughout the Western world, female circumcision is called *mutilation* . . . and it's *fucking outlawed!*

California, Colorado, Delaware, Illinois, Maryland, Minnesota, Missouri, Nevada, New York, North Dakota, Oregon, Rhode Island, Tennessee, Texas, West Virginia, and Wisconsin all ban FGM. In April 1997, it was made a federal crime, punishable by up to five years. And "cultural beliefs or practices" won't get you off the hook, you sick assholes! "You cut your daughter's genitals, you're doing time," sez Uncle Sam.

Wanna slice your boy's dick? Go right ahead, it's a *tradition!*

When both my kids were born, we were surprised by the sex (we chose not to be informed by the ultrasound guy). About ten minutes before my first daughter was born, the OB/Gyn said to me "So if it's a boy, I'll circumcise him, right?"

"Absolutely not," I answered.

The doctor went ballistic and threw all kinds of completely invalid "medical" reasons at me from hygiene to cervical cancers linked to male foreskins.

I got really pissed and bellowed at him about his bogus bullshit and he backed off.

Even the AAP (American Academy of Pediatrics) says there's no compelling medical reason for circumcision.

I had a Labrador retriever. He was uncircumcised. He never got an infection, he never got penis cancer, he pissed gallons a day, and I watched him hump any number of bitches in heat and both parties seemed to enjoy themselves immensely.

The last and by far lamest reason people circumcise is they don't want little Hunter to feel *different*. If little Hunter is doing johnson comparisons in the locker room, he's gonna be more *different* than his foreskin could ever make him.

Lastly, some guys have actually had themselves circumcised in adulthood. Most regret it, claiming that sex was way better with their original equipment. (Doctors estimate that as much as 50 percent of sensitivity is lost with the removal of the foreskin.) Alas, it's not a reversible procedure. What it is, is barbaric mutilation. Having outlawed it for females but not males is a clarion call to all MACK DADDIES to rise up and correct this biased, sexist, bigoted, and discriminatory legislation.

Write or e-mail your congressman today, and leave your baby's dick *intact!*

Experiences to Savor

Remember to ask the Ob/Gyn to let you cut the umbilical cord. Both times, the doc offered me the scissors first—it's really so kooky. What's shocking is the girth of the thing. I expected it to be like bakery-box string. In fact, it's more like a pumpkin stem. Start working your handgrips a month before—it takes some effort to cut through it.

While all this stuff is happening, the staff will be giving your kid its APGAR tests (one minute old and already a pop quiz?). It's actually simple stuff—they check her pulse, respiration, reflexes, color, and overall activity. They check her at one minute old and again at five minutes, just to be sure everything is going okay. I don't recall getting a report card.

If you like to shoot pictures (as I do), you face a bit of a delivery-room dilemma. You want to get great shots, but if you watch the action through a viewfinder, you may feel as if you missed it. There are some standard photo ops you can plan for, allowing you to be more "in the moment."

When the baby is born, you can have the doc cheese it as he hefts him for you. (No, they don't hold it up by its feet and slap its ass.) Then, they'll usually put the baby right on Mommy's chest. Another Kodak moment. Then there's the weigh-in—a nice archival shot. There's a little table with warm lights like in a hamburger joint. They usually put him there for a while, too. With both our children, my wife's labor spanned two shifts, so we had a couple of different labor nurses. They were both terrific, and I took pictures of them with Irene for the album.

They'll put a wrist band on your baby and match them up with yours and Mommy's so there's no mix-ups. The wristband has a chip in it that trips an alarm should someone try exiting the hospital with your kid.

Once the baby is born, they clear you out of the delivery room pretty fast, so take a minute or three to just drink in the enormity of what's happened. While you're at it, you might also try to reconcile the miracle you've just witnessed as being the accidental end-product of some cosmic kaboom a few billion light years ago. If the big bang theory looks pretty idiotic right about now, that's because it *is*.

If you haven't settled on a name (as we hadn't), when you see your baby's face the right choice may become obvious.

Some people make the delivery room into a party. They invite friends and relatives, send out for pizza, blast a boom box.

After the delivery room, it's off to the hospital room for your wife. Some hospitals take the baby to the nursery—another photo op. With our second baby, they had those hamburger lights on a rolling cart and wheeled her right into the room so Irene could nurse her. It's such a strange and fantastic feeling to sit there with this brand-new person who, ten minutes earlier, you didn't know. Now, you would gladly give an eye, kidney, or your life for her.

Mom will stay with baby overnight, so now's your chance to hit the 8-Ball Club for a few lap dances—just kidding. Unless you're Steve Stamina, you'll be lucky not to fall asleep on the drive home. When you get there, there will be a hundred messages on the answering machine.

If you can manage it, that night is a good time to do whatever's needed to make Mom and baby comfortable when you bring them home. You can stock the changing table, assemble the bassinet, make the beds, whatever. Remember, she's had it tougher than you, so gallantry is de rigueur.

Even people who work in hospitals will tell you—hospital food is shit. On your way back there to visit New Mom, pick up some of her favorite grub (for Irene it was a corned beef on rye and potato salad)—she'll love it. Don't forget the flowers and IT'S A BOY/GIRL balloons. Throw her a call before you leave the house to be sure she doesn't need something she forgot to pack—hair brush, fuzzy slippers, bathrobe.

Don't forget the baby car seat! Many hospitals send a nurse to escort you to your car and watch you buckle your bambino in. That precaution did nothing to ensure the motoring safety of my first child. For weeks, we buckled her into the car seat improperly. Only after my sister-in-law saw a snapshot of Olivia in transit were we apprised of our faulty buckling technique. If you have a friend with a baby, check out their buckling method in advance.

When you pick up your wife and baby, they'll have a nurse drop by her room to give you a few tips. A lot of her rap is pretty funny, like *don't have sex for six weeks, if your breasts become engorged put ice on them, don't do housework, don't drive for two weeks* yeah, yeah, blah, blah. After she finishes her monologue, be sure to get what *you* need out of her. Make her *show* you how to swaddle the baby. Ask her advice on feeding times, rocking, bathing—as much as you can think of—it's her job and she'll gush all day.

They bring a wheelchair for Mom (this is for insurance purposes), put the baby in her arms, and you get to wheel her out to the parking lot. Look at your baby's face! It's his first view of the world. Imagine how he feels.

Think you drove carefully the first time you piloted your shiny new ride from a showroom? Wait till you've got a baby on board. You'll want to install phaser shields. When you look in the rearview mirror and see that tiny, angelic face . . . wow.

Kiddie Car Seats—A Conveyance Conundrum

It's amazing how many people still don't wear seat belts. Why is that? When they climb aboard the Tilt-a-Whirl or the Insta-Puke Upside-Down Death Coaster, do they tell the goon running the ride, *Hey, leave this friggin' safety bar offa me—fuck gravity. I'll take my chances!*

Get the car seat *before* the baby is born.

Kiddie car seats are actually fantastic lifesavers. Though they must meet government specs, you should still shop around for what's best for you. Most come with a base that you buckle in and leave there. Then, the actual seat is removable. You can pull these out, leaving the kid strapped in and plop it onto a shopping cart or its own stroller, without waking baby (that's a beautiful thing). You'll spend some time lugging it by hand, so be sure to get the one with a handle that has an S curve in it, otherwise you're a cinch for rotator cuff pain after the first quarter mile.

Once the baby is in the seat, there is a shoulder harness with a plastic slider. Make sure to slide it up high on her chest, or else she'll fly out of the harness the first time you stop short.

Many of those kiddie car seats are multitaskers, called *Combos,*

Convertibles, or *Travel Systems*. They tend to suck. Products that try to do many things are usually good at none *(it's a wok, it's a phone, it's an earth-mover!)*. We had a kiddie car seat that snapped into its own stroller. It worked pretty good for the first kid, so we kept it in the garage and dusted it off for the second. I was crossing a busy street with it, and the designed-by-a-moron hunk o' shit collapsed! Had there been traffic, my month-old daughter and I might have been road kill. When I examined the thing later on, the flange that kept it in the open position was made of flimsy plastic that folded for no reason other than its fragile material and half-assed design.

Get a car seat that's just a car seat. Some of them sell the seats and bases separately. An extra base can be a time saver if you run around in more than one car.

Pretty soon, the baby outgrows the infant car seat. Then you trade up for the kiddie car seat. Check with your local DMV about these things, as different states have different laws about how old the kid must be, whether it faces forward or rear-ward, when you can down grade to a simple booster seat, how much the kid can weigh, and so forth.

The aesthetics are as nutty as you can imagine—Karakoram Adventure styles, Star Wars, you name it (funny, they don't make any Maxim cover babe models—guess the mommies find those a little threatening). Even Recaro, the racing seat guys who've custom-made ass-buckets for dozens of Indy and Lemans champs, now have a frigging seat for baby.

If you care about appearance, get one in which the liner is easily removed. Your kid will eat, drink, piss, puke, and shit in it—might as well be machine washable. Some have cup holders, some have storage compartments and netting—they probably make one in camo for the Humvee survivalist freaks.

Whatever the style, bells, or whistles, don't forget to strap the little darling into it each and every time you go for a ride. More than once, I put my child into the seat, drove to my destination, and found her unbuckled in it. Kids have a way of distracting you.

Of course, MACK DADDIES are hip to vehicular maintenance and only run dyna-tuned, road-worthy rides. But it's amazing how many of those *other* daddies obsess over baby's car seat, yet the shit-heap they buckle it into has bald/under-inflated tires, worn brake pads, crumbling wiper refills, windshield cracks, and worse—they drive like assholes, mindlessly yakking away on their cell phones, oblivious to the semi about to T-bone them at the next crossroads.

People obsess over childproofing their homes, over terrorist attacks, and rogue meteors, but odds are, if mayhem befalls you, it will be in your car. Vigilance, baby, vigilance!

Chapter 4

1–3 Months

Exploiting Fatherhood for Financial/ Personal Gain

Fatherhood is the most pivotal event in your life. The first cry of your baby is tantamount to the crack of a starter's pistol in a nearly endless marathon without rules or route. But make no mistake about it, you are in a race. Unless you are the very fortunate beneficiary of a generous trust fund, you'll be more success motivated than ever.

Your apartment, condo, or house will suddenly be too small. And if not now, by the time your baby is ready for school, the local school will be too dangerous, too far, or academically inferior.

Odds are, your boss and his or her boss and the person running or owning the company have a family, and therefore, it would behoove you to make it very well known around the office that you are now a family man. Get a picture of that bambino on your desk. Better still, get one of Mommy holding her. On "take your kid to work day"—be sure you do. You know how competitive things are, use every advantage you have. And no, it is *not* a sympathy ploy.

The fact is a guy with several mouths to feed is far less likely to run off with a belly dancer in the middle of the corporate merger.

Guys with families are perceived as being more reliable, dedicated, and even loyal to the company. If a better gig opens up with a company on another coast, who is more likely to grab it? The guy who has to sell a house and uproot his kids or the single man or woman?

If you do work for a big company, start investigating before your kid's birth as to what perks they offer for families. Some can be pretty generous.

Once your kid is born, keep up the "awareness campaign." Freshen the desk picture every now and then. Better still, make a slide show screen saver out of your kid's pictures and make sure the screen faces the door when you leave the office. No one would ever dare give you static about that.

When your four-year-old has a ballet recital, send an invitation to your bosses. You know damn well they won't attend, but it might be remembered come raise time. Whatever you do, *do not* brag about your kid's brain power, pitching arm, snowboarding, beauty, wise-cracks, or APGAR scores. Nothing, but *nothing* makes people hate you *and* your kid faster than having to listen to you extol their virtues. Do all your campaigning silently.

When you see your boss's kid in a picture on his desk, don't fail to comment on how handsome, bubbly, smart, whatever his kid is. He or she will love to hear that shit, even though the kid is as ugly as a bucket of elbows.

Do not, repeat do not, bring your kid in to canvass the office when he's selling chocolate bars for the school. People will not appreciate you pimping him around the office, and no MACK DADDY would ever consider selling the stuff *for* his kid. It's a real quick way to brand yourself a low-rent rube.

Baby's Drinking Problem and
Your 6-Step Program

Some babies can chug like a frat brother with a beer bong. Then, they'll conk out for 12–14 straight hours. Others resemble dowagers at a tea party . . . petite sips, then, the vapors or whining.

If your kid fits the latter profile, that's tough, but it can be overcome. Lotsa folks call it colic, a catch phrase for an infant who's generally a pain in the ass for no particular reason. Actually, there *are* reasons, but none of the damn runts can properly articulate them. Most pediatricians ascribe it to a supposition that some kids' stomachs are more adaptable to breast milk or formula while others still crave the umbilical cord.

My first daughter was definitely a chugger. She would guzzle a full bottle, belch like an elephant seal, and hibernate. Daughter #2 was colicky. Experimentation was in order. When Mommy fed her, that was between the two of them. But when it was Pop's turn with the bottle, I nearly went insane. She'd take a few sips, then jerk her head like she was drowning, and cry. I'd straighten her up and try all my best burping moves. She'd burp (or fart) and then cry for the bottle. Two more sips, same routine, Groundhog Day. Thirty minutes of this and you're ready to spontaneously combust.

After about 2 months of hell, my wife figured it out. The baby's real problem wasn't feeding, it was sleep deprivation. Accustomed to the instant slumber of the first baby, who could sleep on a flagpole in a hurricane, we figured the second was just an insomniac. Wrong. She just needed more cuddling and rocking to get to sleep. Once she started sleeping more, the feedings got easier; the crying diminished by 90 percent, and life resumed a semblance of normalcy.

That was until she was ready for baby food. Just when we got the bottle battle won, she hit us with her next barrage. With every spoonful of baby food she'd eat (regardless whether it was applesauce, peas, turkey, or yogurt) she'd scream. This did not augment the quiet, Zen-like ambience we try to maintain at the dinner table. What was her problem? Sore throat? Hates baby food? Hates spoons? TMJ? We were baffled. She swallowed each spoonful, so obviously, the food was palatable. We thought that perhaps she was so greedy—any time her mouth wasn't full, she'd yell. After weeks, we figured it out. She wanted the spoon. She was teething and enjoyed the feel of the hard spoon in her mouth and got pissed off every time it was removed. Answer: two spoons. One for eating and one for chewing. Her mouth is plenty big enough for both.

AA has a 12-step program; you may find the MACK DADDY 6-step (who has time for 12?) feeding program helpful: nipple, timing, temperature, environment, contents, and position.

1. **Nipples.** They come in three basic configurations. One hole—which, while making the little punk work for every mouthful, reduces overloaded mouths and choking or upchucks. The three-hole variety is a nice middle-ground for moderate drinkers. The crosscut is tantamount to shotgunning formula. If your kid has a gullet like a pelican, crosscut is for you. Try all three and see which minimizes static.
   Note: Nipples wear out. If you turn a bottle upside down and milk leaks out, the nipple is worn out.

2. **Timing.** This is truly a trial-and-error thing, but babies do thrive more with a routine. They have amazingly accurate internal clocks. Try to feed it around the same time and number of times each day. (My second daughter would hiccup inside Mommy every night at 10 p.m. Her belly looked liked Alien was about to burst through. After she was born, she continued her 10 p.m. hiccup schedule.)

3. **Temperature.** Even the chuggers prefer warm to cold. So warm that formula up a little and he'll probably like it a lot better.

4. **Environment.** If you'd like your kid to develop bag o' hammers personality, requiring heavy dosages of Ritalin, just leave the stereo and TV on full blast 24/7. This constant visual and audio assault will guarantee a fucked-up kid with feeding problems, sleeping problems, facial ticks, syndromes, and disorders of every stripe. If you'd prefer a more normal child, when it comes to feeding/bed time, put the lights low and kill the TV and stereo. (If the neighbor's dog is yapping, you may split his owner's nostrils with a throwing star.) Quiet and tranquil is the right ambience for getting a bottle into baby's belly.

   Do *not* put the baby in his crib with the bottle. He needs to know that his crib is for sleep, not chow. Also, infant formula is nectar to ants, roaches, and other vermin.

5. **Contents.** There are just a few manufacturers of infant formula. But, they make a bunch of different recipes—with iron, low iron, soy. Ask the pediatrician and experiment.

   They make ready-made, pour-straight-from-the-bottle stuff, and mix-it-yourself powder. The powder is a hell of a lot cheaper. The can comes with a little plastic cup–shovel, and if you mix it according to their specs (4 shovels for each 8 ounces of water) it will be much thinner and less satisfying than the straight-from-the-bottle kind. So, when you mix it by the quart, you can throw in an extra shovel.

6. **Position.** Some babies like to drink on their backs. Some prefer to be sitting up. Some like to lay on their side, approximating the way they glug from Mommy's boob. Experiment.

You Rock, Man . . . How to Burp, Rock, and Get Your Kid to Sleep

Amusement parks serve a primordial need. In utero, life is one long haul on the Tilt-a-Whirl. Inside Mommy, we're subject to rapid drops in altitude, pitch, yaw, vibration, shifts in lighting—it's a pretty good ride. The nearest we can replicate these feelings is with a trip to the local carnival.

Most people overlook this when it's time to rock the baby. They treat the baby as if he's made of wet papier mâché, cradling him delicately with near-imperceptible side-to-side motion. Not only won't that put the kid to sleep, it'll probably piss him off, 'cause he's thinking, *Hey, who do I have to pay to get this ride moving!*

I took my kid-rocking cues from the pediatrician. After he jabbed her ass with a needle, she began to bawl. He swept her off the examining table and gave her a full, fast, 360-degree arm's-length spin and as a finale, a bungee-style free-fall of about two feet. This silenced her immediately. I was surprised at how spirited the ride he gave her was. (It was spirited, not *violent*—a big difference between a good, satisfying, safe ride and shaken-baby syndrome.)

Aping his style that night, I was able to rock my daughter to sleep quite quickly. Here's how to bust the move: Try planting your feet at shoulder width, holding the baby in both arms and swinging (none too slowly) about 180 degrees side to side. A few of those will usually do the job. As you see his eyes slip to half-staff, slow the speed and lessen the arc. At this point you can usually plop him into the bassinet or crib. But some kids are very light sleepers.

Going from your warm arms to the cool bedding can wake them. There are a few easy fixes for this. You could throw the baby bedding in the dryer for a couple of minutes. If you're living large, have your valet or footman hit the baby sheets with a hair dryer. Electric blankets are a stupid idea—would you drape *yourself* in live wire and then take a nice, long leak?

Sometimes, the oldest remedies are the best, like the classic hot-water bottle. They cost around 15 bucks. Just buying them is a pisser because of the way the boxes are labeled—"1-quart, enema bag/douche/hot water bottle." Be sure to ask the blue-haired cashier which is her preferred usage and how best to cleanse it

after you've been multitasking with it. Then get her recommendation on the most comfortable lubricants and nozzles. If she's
young and hot, ask her if she likes wearing tight, white uniforms
and role-playing nurse games.

When it's nap time, first make sure the room is dim and noise is
minimal. Fill 'er up with warm tap water and tuck it in the crib a
few minutes before the rocking routine. Her bed will be plenty
toasty when she's ready to snooze. You can wrap the bag in a
small towel and sandwich it close to her—it can fake her out into
believing Mommy or Daddy is sleeping next to her.

If the hot water bottle gimmick doesn't work, you can try return-
ing it to that same blue-haired cashier. Or, if you're a particularly
buffed MACK DADDY, give this carnival strongman stunt
(actually perpetrated by Franco Columbu, Schwarzenegger's
old gym pal) a shot. Next time your friends and neighbors are
over, whip that bottle out, put it to your lips, and huff and puff
until you explode the son of a bitch. Be sure video is rolling and
remember to close your eyes at ka-boom. Have an ambulance
outside with the engine idling, in case you self-inflict an
aneurysm or burst a lung in the effort.

Here's a major MACK DADDY tip that can save you hours of
fruitless labor. When that baby is in Mom's belly, she is confined.
While she can move, she won't be doing jumping jacks. After
nine months of gentle confinement, babies come to like the
feeling. That's part of the reason they tend to stop crying when
picked up and cuddled. When you put the baby in bassinet or
crib she feels like an astronaut on a space walk—lost and
vulnerable. You can fix this by swaddling her like the Mummy.
But pretty soon, she gets annoyed by the confinement. When
that happens, try putting her on her side, with her back against
the crib bumper. Then, shove a rolled towel or baby blanket
into her chest and torso, so she's supported on both sides.
They manufacture all kinds of exotic, sculpted pillows and
orthopedic-approved cushions that do the same thing as a towel.
Duh.

Burping, while difficult for adults to suppress, actually requires effort for babies. Most need help.

Some seem to burp better in an upright position, slung over the shoulder. Some like it across the knees. For some, gentle back pats get the job done. For others, more effort is required. Some need you to actually massage those air bubbles up the back and out the esophagus.

If your kid's a burper, rejoice. Some prefer to fart. Getting them to fart is trickier and fraught with difficulty. Put the li'l stinker on his back or belly, grab the ankles, and pump those chunky little legs. Doing it outside, in a breeze, might be best. Or have your wife take you for a spin with the top down.

Here's another tip for getting jinky babies to sleep. At bedtime, give her the bottle, then slowly walk to her crib and rock her as she feeds. Then, as she falls asleep, substitute a pacifier for the bottle and gently put her in the crib.

If you have the time, take a tip from a guy who knew—Bob Hope. The wise-cracking centenarian claimed the secret of his longevity was a daily massage. Maybe he knew something. Because unlike most people who get really ancient, Bob's later years were productive, active ones—he was still jetting around the world, playing golf, and having his picture taken with hot babes.

Who doesn't like a nice massage? Babies love them and it's a great way to calm them if they're wired or cranky. You can get really elaborate or be Spartan—your choice.

Get a big, soft towel and spread it out on a carpeted floor. Put that naked angel on her back. Make sure no bright lights are in her eyes. Better still, dim the lights and put on some soft music. Squirt a little oil in your hands and warm it up, then just follow your instincts and see what kind of rub she likes best. You can start with her shoulders and squeeze and rub her pudgy arms. Then work your way across her chest, belly, and her legs. You can talk to her or sing, ask her how she plans to vote in '28 and where she thinks hemlines will be this fall. You'll be amazed at how well your baby will respond. Then, turn her over and work her little back, butt, legs, and feet. Even when her face is on her side, you'll see the expression of satisfaction. Sometimes she'll conk out before you're finished. It's a terrific way to bond with her, too.

Talkin' Shit: Disposables vs. Cloth Diapers

The debate has raged for decades. And still, no one has a definitive answer. No question, disposables are easy and portable. But, the tree huggers say shame, shame, and claim non-degradable disposables sit in landfills for centuries and cost untold tons of trees and petroleum products to manufacture. That all makes sense.

Then they say all that infant pee pee and poo poo enters landfills untreated and may contaminate ground water supplies. *Ding ding!!! Reality check, please!* Isn't that the way cesspools and leaching pools work, and often a few yards from well water? What about the millions of heads of livestock peeing and dumping onto the land? Why hasn't all that ground water been contaminated? So campers, do *not*, repeat, do *not* piss in the woods. Instead, all urine shall be saved in containers and brought to the urine treatment center so we can make it *safe*.

The pro-disposable guys say, hey, what about all the fresh water wasted in washing those shit-filled cloth diapers? And the fossil fuel burned to heat the water? Aren't diapers made from cotton? How about all farming equipment used to grow that cotton? And ground-water contaminating manure used to fertilize the cotton fields and the farm hands pissing in those fields and then the looms and bleaches and chemicals at the textile mills and *Oh, mother of God, where does it end?*

For years, we lived near a couple of professional morons. They had two mutts that barked incessantly and left piles of shit all over their concrete yard, which they regularly cleaned up—once or twice a year. Many a summer day, when temps popped to 110+ degrees, both dogs would be outside suffering in the sun all day, barking because the water in their dishes had evaporated by noon. This couple also had two infants, and being environmentally conscientious, two to three times a week, a big, exhaust-spewing truck would deliver fresh dideys and take away the stinky ones to a laundry some 40 miles away. Of course, both "professionals" drove gas-guzzling monster SUVs. Good thing they used cloth diapers. *Save the planet, folks!*

Cloth or disposable, take your pick. But whichever, make sure you're not indulging in environmental hypocrisy.

We opted for disposable and got a bonus mystery with the first kid. One time as I changed her, I thought *Oh, my God, she's eaten something really weird.* Mixed in with her copious dumpus were the strangest looking little green beads. It almost looked like fish roe. It was actually the stuff that soaks up all that pee pee. Those are gel polymer particles, about the size of grains of salt when dry. Once wet, they swell to several times that size and if the diaper tears, you'll think your kid has crapped Martian solid rocket fuel.

But what's best for baby? If you can change that cloth diaper the minute he pees, it's a draw. But on balance, the disposable, with those kooky space-age pee-absorbent beads, will keep that muffin drier longer. *Sorry, Greenpeace.*

Let Your Baby Make You a Strollin' Stud

Guys spend their youth seeking female attention. We burn cash, time, and energy trying to attract and impress women.

Rock and movie stars don't have this problem. With an infant, you won't either.

Memo to Siggy Freud: What do women want? Babies. Women want babies.

The first few months of fatherhood can be trying. Babies cut into everything—sleep, space, peace and quiet, meals. But your baby will give back so much more than he takes—if you know the MACK DADDY secrets.

It's Saturday. Maybe you're thinking about a round of golf . . . wondering how to broach the subject to your wife. How's she going to like the idea? Let's see . . . she's been with that kid 24/7 for the last five days and now you're going to maroon her and baby so you can hang with your pals and chase a white ball with acne pits? This may not fly.

Here's the MACK DADDY play.

"Honey, I bet you could use a break. I'm taking (insert baby's name) out for a few hours. Anything you want me to get while I'm out?"

That'll hit her like a 50-pound box of Godiva. She'll pack the baby bag with all the stuff you need. Within 60 seconds of your exit she'll be on the phone to friends gloating that *her* husband is out with the baby so she can relax, sleep, read, watch a movie, take a bubble bath, whatever. "Isn't he fa-a-a-bulous," she'll gush. Meanwhile, her friends' hubbies are at the links, sports bar, bowling lanes doing the same crap with the same yo-yos just like always.

And where will you be?

At the mall or shopping district—wherever women congregate. You are in possession of the ultimate aphrodisiac—a newborn. When you push that stroller, women—especially young, fertile women—will swarm you like seagulls on a bait raft.

Here's a tip. Once you hit the mall/street, take the baby out of the stroller and hold her face right next to yours. This will make you feel as if all the adoring looks are directed at you.

Soon, one will ask if she can hold your baby. Her face will light up like you just handed her a winning Lotto ticket. Then the questions begin—how old is she? What's her name? Is this your first? And so on.

After a while, you carefully reclaim your chick magnet. That's the moment you need to stay focused for the pay-off. As she's parting with something she wants so very, very badly, it will occur to her to check out the source of the paternal gene-pool—you. She'll be predisposed to liking what she sees. The look you'll get is priceless—usually reserved for movie and rock stars—savor it.

On to the next vortex of maternal need. Don't worry—they'll find you.

It's harmless fun and a fortifying experience. Why shouldn't a proud papa get some adoration from strange women? Dig it. Soak it up. You're entitled.

On your way out of the mall, remember to pick up a trinket for the babe who made these thrills possible—your wife.

- *Caveat I:* As your baby ages, its female-enthralling powers will diminish. Stroll early and often.

- *Caveat II:* What's the most dangerous animal in the jungle? Any female with new cubs. Human females know this and act accordingly.

I recall dining at a favorite restaurant with my wife and newborn daughter. Waitresses would sneak hungry glances at our infant—but none made any comment nor dared get close. Then my wife went to the ladies' room. Instantly, a swarm converged on my daughter, smiling and cooing and touching her feet.

The moment Mommy reappeared, they vanished like spooked fish.

So even when out with baby *and* mommy, stay keen. The fun is everywhere.

Perhaps you have a single friend who'd like to meet more girls. Lend him your kid! It's free babysitting. Once he sees the results he gets, he'll gladly pay *you* for baby rental.

MACK DADDY Regains His Strut

The first few weeks are pretty tough. It takes a while to figure out what your baby wants and when he wants it. Waking up two or three times a night doesn't do much for your outlook when the alarm clock goes off.

But by the three-month mark, you and Mommy should be regaining your equilibrium. That baby should have some semblance of a routine and your life should be getting back on track. Maybe it's time for a little MACK DADDY reward.

Chicks are smart. Learn from them. When life pummels them, how do they self-heal? They get a massage, a manicure, a new outfit, or their hair done—or all four.

Question: How could the Japanese Imperial Army have made the Bataan death march even more horrific?

Answer: By routing it through the mall.

Yeah, shopping sucks. But, after you've dropped the beer gut and sculpted yourself into Mr. Olympia, you'll need some new threads.

Investing a few bucks in some fresh vines ain't a bad idea. Whether you're searching for that new shirt and cravat to wear for the big presentation, or some happenin' duds for strolling your new kid down Main Street, remember these three words:

Buy the Dummy

Retailers, whether big department stores or Gap, Banana Republic, Abercrombie, American Eagle, pay people *handsomely* to dress those mannequins in the window. And since those dummies are the only way to lure you into the store, they don't let some cashier or stock boy take a whack at it. They use *pros*. And those pros sort through that store's entire inventory to find the slickest, hippest, chick-magnetic clothing. And that's what they put on the dummies.

Then what do those other idiot dads do? They walk in and buy a purple Hawaiian shirt so vile, it could make a luau pig vomit on it. They buy some crap that professional mannequin dresser wouldn't use to polish his car. If you buy the dummy, people will assume you have the GQ touch.

- Lactating Daddy gets shirts with nipple flaps for breast-feeding on the fly.

- Der Fuehrer Daddy only wears official regulation jerseys from his fave pro ball franchise, or military surplus, presenting himself to the world as an aged water boy or a corporal AWOL from the idiot's army. Unless your physique resembles that of a pro athlete, leave the sports getups to kids and real athletes.

- Rubber-Stamp Daddy buys and wears whatever his wife tells him to buy.

- Daddy Distant swathes himself *only* in corporate logo-wear. This means pastel polo/golf shirts and pleated khakis with cuffs as big as the map pockets in his Volvo wagon. Since it is a uniform of sorts, its saves him the trouble of finding his own clothing.

If you want to take no chances, just find the niche clothier that best suits your personality and body style and buy their dummy, head to toe.

Want folks to think that when you're not at the office, you're cranking a winch on your 12-meter racer? Buy the Nautica Dummy.

Need a facade of old money to prop up your image? Ralph Lauren's polo player dummy to the rescue.

Fancy yourself more of a contemporary urban patriarch? Buy the Sean John dummy. And so on. Of course, if you have the cake, you can go the "personal shopper" route, but even they aren't as talented as the dummy dressers.

Go Out to Eat . . . *Now!*

New parents bitch and moan about infants. They cry, they wake you up at night, they're high maintenance. It's all true. But babies also sleep a lot—some as much as 20, 21 hours a day. And at that young age, they sleep *deep*. But, it's an ever-narrowing window of opportunity, because the older they get, the less they sleep.

New parents also complain of never getting a chance to go out at night, of being imprisoned by that baby. In fact, if you work out the routine, you can salvage your evenings. If you've got him in the right groove, you can keep up your nocturnal bowling/softball/AA/whirling dervish/gourmand obligations. Just tuck him in that kiddie car seat—and go. You'll be amazed how naturally it will fit into the banquette at your favorite bistro.

When our first baby was about three weeks old, Irene and I could no longer squelch our craving for a Mexican feed. The baby conked out about five thirty for what we knew would be at least a three-hour nap, so away we went to our fav' taco house.

We carried her in her car seat, plopped it up on a barstool between us, and knocked back a couple of frozen Margaritas while we waited for our table. (The imbecile/zero tolerance barkeep had some beef about *no one under 21* at the bar—I told him it wasn't a *real* baby, but a realistic new doll we were test-marketing.) Soon, we were shown to a table and devoured a gut-pleasing meal of Yucatan delights. The baby slept through everything. Once we discovered this little secret, we went out as much as possible—restaurants, museums, concerts in the park— pretty much everywhere but movies.

So take advantage of your infant's long and deep napping habits. Even when he wakes you can usually keep him happy for a while with a bottle or pacifier. Live it up . . . *while you can.*

Once that baby can crawl, it gets a lot tougher. When they get tired, they get cranky.

In a matter of seconds, they can ramp up from fidgety to whiney to crying to a five-alarm, back-on-the-floor flailing limbs, top-o'-the lungs shrieking meltdown. And won't that make for a pleasant dining experience?

The Four-Star Take-Out Experience

Here's a gimmick you can use when getting out to eat just isn't feasible: the Four-Star Take-Out Experience. The play is this. Feed the kid a little early and get him bedded for the night. Phone your favorite take-out joint and order a feast (Italian or Chinese may work best for this). While your order is en route, lay the fancy china, linens, and silverware on the dining table. Spark a couple of candles. Throw some Frank or Dean on the stereo. Lower the lights. When the chow arrives, get it out of cardboard and onto the plates chop-chop. Uncork a nice bottle of vino. You may be amazed how enjoyable talking to your wife is when you don't have to sneak in sentences between your baby's squawks.

After a recent Four-Star Take-Out Experience, our five-year-old gave us static the morning after when she spotted Italian leftovers in the fridge.

Pointing at candles on the table, "You ate a secret dinner without me," she charged. "How could you *do* that?"

"Sometimes Daddy and I need to eat alone so we can think of new ways to make your life more wonderful," Irene offered.

Olivia's squinty, sidelong glance proved that even at five, kids *get* sarcasm.

From Whence Father's Day?

Of course, it just had to be started by some daddy's little girl, in this case one Sonora Smart Dodd (nice handle!) of Spokane, Washington. She staged a fiesta for her daddy (who raised six kids solo, after the untimely demise of his wife) on June 19, 1910.

In 1924, Cal Coolidge got behind the idea. In '66, LBJ proclaimed Father's Day a national holiday, and in '72 Nixon officially nailed it as the third Sunday of June.

It's the fifth most popular card-selling holiday, tied with Easter (3%) and trailing Mother's Day (4%), Valentine's Day (25%), and Christmas (60%).

That measly 3 percent generates almost $100 million in card sales each year. God knows how many disgusting neckties and bottles of Old Spice are moved as well, but the leading dad gift categories are apparel (41%), dinner (38%), sporting goods (22%), home improvement stuff (18%), electronics (17%), and gardening tools (12%).

Chapter 5

3-12 Months

The Fun Quotient Increases

Somewhere around the three-month mark (and don't get tense if he's a few months later, or if earlier, don't go contacting Mensa) you'll see some major changes in the baby. For those first three months, that kid is pretty much sleeping or nursing, or crying because she needs either. Then, a person—with a personality—begins to emerge. It's the most exciting, glorious thing to watch.

The baby begins to smile. If you work at it, you can make him laugh. (My older daughter's first laugh was extracted by her aunt Jeannine. I was determined to be the reason for my second daughter's maiden chuckle.) Don't bother tickling; that can be a little cruel and is for amateurs. Try making faces, rubbing his little Buddha belly, or giving him short parachute drops. These are the days when you really want to keep the camcorder charged up with a fresh tape.

By this time, you can interpret the nuances of their cries, being able to distinguish among *I'm hungry, I'm tired, I have to burp/fart,* and *I have a load in my diapers.* Then, they also begin to coo, growl, mew, and I swear, attempt speech. Jackie, my youngest daughter, would actually echo the sounds we made, in pitch and duration. You could see the little tongue in her big mouth moving, and that call and recall of extended sounds was uncanny.

Imagine what it will be like to hear your child's first word. What will it be? Olivia's was *bird*. There were always doves nesting on our deck—we'd show her the chicks in the nest (which, by the way, freeze like statues until you go away—they're a day or two old and already have defense mechanisms). One morning, as we sat outside with her, she pointed her pudgy, crooked baby finger at a dove, looked at us and said *burr*. What a thrill!

Then, the race was on for the utterance of the most important word of all—would it be Mama or Dada? She proved herself to be Daddy's little girl, when, not long after *burr*, she stood in her crib and called *Da-da!*

Besides smiling and laughter, you'll see some other pretty cool behaviors. She'll try to grab that baby bottle. She'll smile and hide her face, initiating a game of peek-a-boo. You'll establish routines that if broken will get you a perplexed look. When changing my daughter, she loved to kick the box of wipes. She did it with a vengeance, grinning and laughing. One day the box wasn't there and, kicking the air, she knew something was amiss and pouted. I put the box back in its place, her feet lashed out, and the smile returned.

These are such fabulous times when you can interact with your baby. Don't miss out on carrying her now instead of later when she'll be less cooperative and maybe give you a hernia. I just can't keep my hands off my infant. If she's in my arms, I'm kissing her. On a recent trip to a museum, my wife and I became separated. I had the baby in my arms and my wife located me by following the sounds of incessant kissing. Do I sometimes drive her nuts? Hell yeah, but I figure that's nothing compared to the headaches she has in store for me when she's a teenager.

Around four to five months, some kids start on solid food, and that's another hoot. I had the thrill of feeding my elder daughter her first taste of applesauce. I put a spoonful in her mouth and she ejected it with her tongue. I tried again, but this time her face became animated and her jaw worked, but she still wasn't hip on the process of eating. It just kind of ran down her chin. Three was the charm, though. She began to gobble voraciously, kicking her feet as she did. It was clear she was over infant formula.

At this age, a baby is aware you've placed a hat on her head. She'll lie under a string of plastic toys and play with them and laugh.

Got an office chair that spins? Hold your baby and make a couple of rotations and as you do, watch your baby's eyes. I guarantee you'll laugh your ass off.

By three months, they're ready for fun. Don't miss out!

The Lowdown on High Chairs

High chairs should be purchased with pretty much the same criteria as changing tables.

When my first daughter was old enough for one (around four months), we overpaid (nearly $300) for a super de luxe imported one. It was snowy white and nautical navy blue. It had more positions than the power seat on a Lexus—up/down, tilt, recline. It had a cool vinyl pad with a scalloped backrest. It looked like a midget captain's chair from some mad Italian's yacht. It was an impractical piece of shit.

Why does a high chair need vertical adjustments? Every kitchen/dining table on earth is manufactured to within an inch or two of standard heights. Were we planning on taking our infant to the Japanese teahouse? And that big, cushy vinyl pad with all that stitching was just perfect . . . for trapping rivers of strained beef and bananas. As were the cambers, ratchets, and gears required to facilitate all those tilt, recline, and altitude adjustments.

We realized the error of our ways when we visited Grandma, who picked up *her* high chair for a fraction of what we paid. And it sure was superior. No altitude adjustments, spirit levels, nautilus gears, or Mediterranean-themed cushions. Just a simple plastic chair with a removable tray on four legs. Basic, stable, and easily rendered spotless with a garden hose.

When my second daughter was born, I retrieved the high chair from the garage. As I was cleaning it, it began to crumble, so I tossed it into the garbage. Then I went and bought a great one for $27 (Cosco).

MACK DADDY avoids all bells, whistles, and tricky doo-hickeys. Let's see what those other chumps are buying:

- Lactating Daddy: Has chair custom-built with gamma-ray shields and color-coordinated DOT/Snell approved eating helmet.

- Rubber-Stamp Daddy: Probably hangs with Lactating Daddy, so they order two and get the volume discount

- Der Fuehrer Daddy: Makes infant eat from dog dish until his table manners improve.

- Daddy Distant: Buys the chair with clip for cell phone, in case of *verbal interface*.

Childproofing

The childproofing industry preys on parental hysteria like no other. I've visited homes where paranoid mommas, assisted by Rubber-Stamp or Lactating Daddies, have converted a normal dwelling into a warren of padded cells. Every table corner, ceramic lamp, mantle, and chair arm is wrapped in foam padding.

One childproofing website advises you to *put yourself in your young child's place and crawl around your home on your hands and knees.* If you really want to get inside your toddler's head, why not pull on a Depends, take a long whiz and a hot dump and *then* see what sorta household mischief appeals to you.

The most common causes for injury to kids under five are falls, poisoning, burns, cuts, crushing or trapping (fingers in doors), foreign objects (in ear, nose, eye), car crash, dog bite, choking. The leading causes of *adult* deaths in home "accidents" are falls, poison, fire, suffocation/choking, drowning. Interesting how similar they are, no?

Maybe what we really need is some *adult-proofing*. *Accident* is perhaps the most misused word in our language. When some fool jabbering away on his cell phone drives out of a strip mall without looking and flattens some poor bastard on a Kawasaki—that is *not* an accident—that is a *crash*, caused by an ignorant and negligent asshole. But in this blameless society of victims, everything is an accident . . . until the plaintiff's attorneys have a look at it.

Of course, if you added the filter "alcohol-related" to the stats for accidents, the numbers would be off the charts. MACK DADDIES may drink but they never, *ever* get drunk. That's for the other chumps. MACK DADDIES always have sufficient control of their faculties to help their kids in any emergency. And therefore no emergency ever arises as a result of their impairment.

Most every "accident" is avoidable if you exercise reasonable caution and know where your kid is.

Can you maintain constant visual contact with your kid? Of course not. What you *can* do is limit his access to the more hazardous places in your house. Babies "R" Us sells little kiddie corrals. They're great. You can see the kid, the kid can see you, you can throw in some toys, and while he's in it, you can be certain he won't climb out, hop in the bathtub, and make bubbles with a hair dryer.

Your common sense will carry the day and help your kid attain his majority without maiming or killing himself. Once the baby's crawling, try to eliminate hazards. Don't leave the iron on the board where he can grab the cord and pull a scorching, pointy, five-pound missile onto his skull. Don't leave the straight razor out where he can get it, or the 9mm, for that matter. (A list of things to check would insult anyone but Lactating Daddy's intelligence.) But do you need to convert your home into a bouncy play space?

If you could shield your child from every little injury, you'd be damaging him developmentally. Scraped knees, bee stings, and lumps on the head are a natural part of childhood. Pain is a hell of a teacher.

When my daughter was a young toddler, she developed a taste for waffles. Nana and Papa gave us a waffle iron. Olivia was very curious about it, so I showed it to her and warned her repeatedly never to touch it, as it would hurt her very badly. When my back was turned, she touched it and the tears flowed. It was a very minor burn, but the memory of the ouch lingered—since then she is extremely cautious around barbecues, stoves, and fire of any kind.

Even more important is how *you* react when your child is hurt. If you panic and shriek, you're programming your kid to do the same. If you swoop him up and laugh and say "that's nothing" as you tend to the wound, you show your child that hurt is nothing to fear. This is an absolutely key lesson that will keep your kid strong throughout his life.

Finding Sitters and Nannies—Blindfolded

Think about the talent pool for babysitters. Best of all possible choices? Grandma. But you might live several time zones apart. So you need hired help. Where to find it? The more upscale your address, the tougher and more expensive the search may be.

In parts of L.A. and New York, teenaged girls' allowances exceed doctors' salaries in rural states. Finding one to mind your infant without having to float a home equity loan is not easy.

Our nearest relatives are on the East Coast, so my ever-resourceful wife went to the local university and pinned some help-wanted ads to a bulletin board.

Mind you, the ad was a little juicier than the standard, HELP WANTED: BABYSITTER. We were on deadlines and needed someone to amuse/stroll/read-to our six-month-old daughter while we worked. So there was more cash to be made than a one-night job—making it an easy part-time gig. And being tax-free, it was worth well more than double minimum wage.

Soon, the phone rang. The first applicant arrived wearing a low-cut ruffled shirt, spray-painted-on clam-digger pants, and four-inch spikes. My first thought: *Could be fun watching her play dress-up with my daughter.*

Second thought: *Thoughts like this led Joe Piscopo to divorce court.*

Third thought: *This broad looks like someone who rang the wrong doorbell on her way to a swing party.*

I wondered what Irene was thinking.

Then came my final thoughts regarding this potential sitter: *If, God forbid, there was a fire/earthquake/medical emergency, how fleet of foot would she be in those CFMs? What were the odds of those ruffled sleeves catching fire as she heated a bottle? Of course, the instant they did, my daughter would hit the tiled floor like a Crenshaw melon. There she would remain, writhing in agony until the sitter's sleeves had been extinguished, shirt changed, fresh makeup applied.*

Next.

A gleaming Lexus SUV pulled up, disgorging a well-turned woman in her late thirties and her teenage daughter. With matching Piagets, salon-fresh coiffures, and makeup I thought: *Maybe someone transcribed Irene's index card ad to a website for The OC auditions.*

The doorbell rang.

"Hi! I'm Melissa and this is my daughter Chloe. We're here about the babysitting job?"

"We?"

"Oh, Chloe's Z is being detailed, so I thought I'd give her a lift."

BMW'Z or Nissan Z, I wondered. Did it matter? What's a few thousand $$ sticker swing between friends anyway?

They entered the house. Olivia was in her corral in the living room. Melissa threw one Jimmy Choo'd foot over the fence and hefted Olivia. Chloe stood near the door like she was part of a Hazmat team. Melissa carried Olivia to Chloe. I flashed on some terrifying baby-napping scam, and got between them and the door.

"Mmm. Isn't she beautiful, Chloe?" asked Melissa.

Chloe regarded my daughter as if she were powdered in anthrax. Her mom seemed determined to get the kid interested in babies. Why? Was Chloe out nightly, banging guys at will, and this was the show-and-tell part of her *see what can happen* lecture? Was Chloe some profligate spender, and Mommy was here to show her how hard making a buck really could be? Irene cut short my reverie as she extracted Olivia from Melissa's arms with a casting agent's toothy grin and a "Thanks so much . . . we'll be in touch!"

Melissa and Chloe got the hint and vanished.

Before we could process what had just happened, our final respondent arrived. She drove a beat-up Escort and looked every inch the struggling student, although she had one of those faces that could have made her 19 or 35. It was hard to tell. Since we only needed her to watch/occupy Olivia while we were at home working, we didn't get into any CIA-caliber background checks. We called her references and hired her.

As time went by, we learned that Mary Beth was somewhere on a seven-year plan to obtaining her two-year degree. While Olivia was already growing bored with Teletubbies, Mary Beth would stay tuned to "see how it turned out." Okay, so she wasn't a rocket scientist, or even a forklift operator, but after two or three months, she seemed pretty competent at minding our daughter.

A wedding invitation forced us to let Mary Beth mind Olivia solo. She was a year old, seemed to enjoy Mary Beth's company, and away we went to Santa Monica. A friend of Irene's was getting hitched at a very toney beach club in a sunset ceremony—the vast, foaming Pacific serving as backdrop as they exchanged vows.

After a couple of hours (about 7:30 p.m.) Irene called home to see how things were going.

No answer.

"She's probably in the middle of putting Olivia down and didn't want to pick up. Try again in ten minutes," I offered.

Ten minutes elapsed. Still no answer. Irene's face turned ashen. I called a friend who lived near my house. He raced over with his key and called me back from inside my house.

"There's no one here. Her car is parked outside."

What was going on? It was now dark, and at least an hour past my 12-month-old baby's bedtime. We were getting frantic.

We left the wedding and hauled ass up Pacific Coast Highway toward our home. Irene kept punching redial on the cell phone. And praying.

Finally, at a quarter past nine, she answered. There was a catch in Irene's throat. Mary Beth had decided to take a walk to the mall. The mall is over a mile away, along unlit streets where packs of coyotes frequently patrol.

You pay someone to watch your child and put her to bed on time; not to take a two-mile hike to a strip mall in the dark of night. We never got a straight answer from Mary Beth as to why she did this. The book she was reading at the time was *Dating for Dummies*. I suspect she was cruising some pimply-faced stock boy at the supermarket. Hell, maybe she fucked him in the produce section while my daughter watched from her stroller.

After this incident, our social life rarely exceeded the boundaries of our yard. For the longest time, it was DVDs and entertaining friends at home.

Cabin fever threatened to destroy us. A friend recommended her sitter. We met Cassandra, liked her immediately, and entrusted Olivia to her.

When we returned home at about midnight, Cassandra, some friend of hers, and our daughter were all up and watching *The Sweetest Thing*—a really stupid movie with its centerpiece sight gag of some skank getting her lip ring snared on the cock-ring of some other cretinous thespian.

So, there came the next lesson. No matter how highly recommended the sitter, lay down the ground rules before you exit the house. No guests. Only videos and DVDs from *your* collection. No walks to the mall. They need to understand the main thing is to get your kid to sleep and then stand by to whisk him from the house in case of fire, flood, or other act of God. Many think that if your child is merely uninjured upon return, they've done their job. Wrong.

There was an interesting case a few years ago and an old but valid bromide that caps its telling. Together, they will guide you through all decisions regarding your child and sitters, nannies, preschool governesses, et al.

A woman was waiting in line at a bus station with her toddler. She asked someone to watch her child while she left the area for a few moments. When she returned, her child was gone as was the perfectly "nice" person who agreed to watch her.

Put this in perspective: If you had a million dollars in cash, would you hand it to a stranger in a bus depot while you stepped outside for a smoke?

Here are a few more tips for navigating the babysitter minefield. Before interviewing someone at your home, prescreen them over the phone. Ask for a few references and call them. Put a list of questions together in advance. Does the sitter know CPR? Worked with kids before? Have younger siblings?

With a new sitter, lay out all the rules as if she just set foot on earth that day. Be ultra clear and specific about everything.

Go with your gut. If you get a wrong vibe off a sitter, don't hire her!

Once you've found a sitter, for the first sitting, have her come to your home a half-hour before you depart. Walk her through the drill—show her the changing table, diapers, wipes, and bottle formula. Be with her and your child. Let them get comfortable with each other. (Some parents have the sitter arrive after the child is asleep—when he awakes, he's in the company of a stranger and terrified—not a good idea!)

Let a neighbor know you have a new sitter and ask if he'll keep an eye on your place. Our neighbor told us one sitter spent half the evening *outside* the house, smoking and talking on her cell phone!

Leave your cell phone number and emergency numbers in plain sight—written large and taped next to the telephone. Then, once you've begun your evening out, call in a couple of times just to see what's happening.

Coping with PBS

What's PBS? It's Pissed-off Baby Syndrome. And when that infant is pissed, unless you can get him un-pissed with alacrity, you'll be popping Advils like Cheetos. Some kids are upfront and telegraph the source of their misery quite clearly. Others make you play Sherlock Holmes. And as with Sherlock, deductive reasoning will carry the day.

There's generally only one reason the baby is pissed off, and that's physical. He hasn't had a shitty day at the office, fought with his girlfriend, or watched a plunging Nasdaq decimate his portfolio. So when he goes into meltdown mode and his mouth looks like it could sheathe a volley ball, start asking yourself some questions. When was his last nap, and was it long enough? Is his belly full? Does he need to burp or fart? Has he been strapped into that stroller in the same position for so long his vertebrae are fusing? Is his diaper full or soaked? Is the sun burning him blind? Is he sweating? Is he cold? Is he teething?

Next, start looking for secondary physical reasons. Here, you need to think outside the box and have 20/20 vision. Did a bug bite him? Is there the stub of a sales ticket embedded in his clothes that's jabbing him? Does he have a rash? Are his clothes too tight? Is there something pointy between his ass and the car seat/stroller-back/high chair? Maybe it's that heinous Neil Young song on the radio.

Once you've exhausted those possibilities, you have to really dig deep. My pal's infant was miserable all the time. He'd tear at his clothes as he whined and cried. It was insufferable and unstoppable. He washed the baby's clothes in fragrance-free, hypoallergenic detergents. Still the kid cried and tore at them. He cut off all the care labels and examined the outfits for any irritants. It didn't help. The only time the kid was calm was when stripped to his diapers—somewhat impractical in a New York winter. Finally, he did the Sherlock schtick and took a powerful magnifying glass to his baby's garments. There he found many teeny, tiny wooden splinters. Where were *those* coming from? Answer: The cheap-shit furniture he'd been given to hold baby's wardrobe. Though made of fairly nice wood, the drawers had particle-board bottoms. The top sides had a smooth lacquer finish, but the *undersides* were unfinished and that's where all those .15 millimeter splinters were coming from. That poor kid spent his first few months like some masochist monk in a hair shirt—and pants!

Another friend solved a case of PBS that was pretty funny. On a four-mile jog behind the stroller, his 16-month-old began screaming as he held his right hand pressed to his tiny side. Dad asked himself all the right questions, but still the baby screamed.

And the hand pressed to the side was really worrisome. The jog became a sprint for home as the baby's screams grew louder. Do babies get appendicitis? Was his spleen ruptured from a rough ride?

Once home, his cooler-headed wife grabbed the baby's hand and forced it away from his side. The hand was stuck there—palm down—by a huge gob of snot he must have pulled from his honker and slapped on his abs. It dried like Krazy Glue and scared hell out of him.

Lastly, there can be some psychological reasons for a kid to wig. Both my younger daughter and her cousin went through a stage where they would freak if Mommy left their sight, even for a second. A kid can be terrified by someone's voice, or a noise (again, think Neil Young), or a large, unfamiliar person suddenly looming over them. (Imagine waking in the night to find Shaquille O'Neal spread-eagled on your ceiling, wordlessly glaring at you.)

Babies actually are articulate in their own way. After a short while, you'll be able to distinguish the reasons for their cries. Hunger is pretty distinct. So is fatigue. *Lemme outta my crib* has its own tone and cadence. *I've fallen and I'm scared shitless* has a unique sound. Usually preceded by a thud, there's a two- to three-second silence that's actually a lung-filling inhale to fuel an ear-splitting cry. (If you hear a thud but no cry, get ready to dial 911 and pray.) Then there's that colicky wail that's pretty similar to *I'm hungry*. If any of these cries go unanswered, you'll notice they become tinged with anger. The voice becomes rougher, volume increases, and breath-catching intervals are longer.

When you pick the baby up, the cries may stop—for lemme *outta my crib*. But if it's any of the other reasons, attend to it quickly—a baby screaming in your ear will make you deaf.

Some parents believe babies need to just "cry it out." That's okay when your baby is over-tired. He's missed a nap, but his belly is full, his diaper is clean, and he's crying. He's just so off his routine, so he wails for a while. But if he doesn't conk out after a few minutes, it's probably something else.

Ailments and Dealing with Doctors

Babies, especially breast-fed ones, have fabulous immune systems and rarely become ill. But when they do, you're looking at a major challenge. They can't tell you what's troubling them, so you and your pediatrician must figure it out.

The first time babies get sick, it's usually a common cold, often bestowed upon them by an older sibling who picked up her dose at nursery school. What are you in for? More sleep loss. First thing you'll notice is a steady stream of green goo dripping from those tiny nostrils. She'll also be cranky and whiny. Check for fever with that high-end digital thermometer. A rectal temp is most accurate (and tough to get)—but under the arm won't be too far off.

If she's running a fever, call the doctor. If he doesn't have you bring her to the office, he'll probably tell you to give her some Infant Tylenol. It comes in fruit flavors. You draw the proper dosage into an eyedropper, put it between her tongue and cheek, and squirt. They make a variety that helps with coughs and congestion as well. Until the baby gets that medicine, you won't be getting sleep. Most babies sleep with their mouths closed. When the nose clogs up, they freak out and cry. Here's where that snot sucker comes in. She can't blow her nose, so you can give a little help. She should lose the cold in a couple of days.

Unfortunately, there are endless other ailments that can befall an infant. A MACK DADDY medical corollary: **Always get a second opinion; if surgery is involved, get several.** When my daughter was barely two, she developed a scary-looking lump on her chest. Our pediatrician took a look and referred us to his go-to guy, a pediatric surgeon. Unfortunately, he was on vacation.

The damn thing seemed to be growing by the day, so we sought more immediate opinions. The situation rapidly degenerated into a nightmare. A grand total of seven different specialists examined her, and *all* had conflicting opinions. After checking her, one bozo began to scribble instructions on his clipboard. He was making arrangements for surgery the following day. I asked him what he thought the growth was. "I dunno," he arrogantly droned without looking up. "We'll find out after I remove it." I told him he could finish his work-study program with someone else's kid.

Here's another MACK DADDY corollary: **Guys who *really* know their trade know it *cold*.** A genuine 7th-Avenue garmento can eyeball your sport coat, and in one glance, tell you the thread count and whether the seams are hand-stitched or fused. Ditto a competent plumber, mechanic, computer geek, or the dude stacking cantaloupes in the produce section. When an alleged expert stops, stares, and vamps dialog, cut your losses. Leave and find an authentic expert.

We decided to wait until the go-to doctor was back in town. He was clear eyed, steady handed, and exuded confidence. Proving the corollary, he pushed aside my daughter's shirt and said, "Oh yeah, that's a (some variety of cyst I can't recall). It's no big deal. I removed two of these from kids last month." He got the job, and did it magnificently. She barely has a scar.

Fortunately, most early childhood ailments are easily dealt with. But when something more threatening crops up, here's another tip: **Referrals are worthless. Get a *recommendation*.** Doctors will usually give you several referrals. They may be golf buddies, school chums, or merely sawbones with whom he has a reciprocal deal. Press him harder. Ask him: *Which one of these guys would you let take a scalpel to your kid?* You'll get a much more honest answer. And, you'll discover an interesting, unspoken MACK DADDY code. Most fathers love their kids *madly*. And when their kids are referenced, most dads will cut the bullshit and be straight with you. It's a fraternity of a sort.

Dealing with Oracles

Don't people just love to give unsolicited advice and opinions? Ask your wife if, during her pregnancy, she wasn't deluged by other women telling her *You're carrying high and out front, it's a boy.* Or, *You're carrying wide and low, it's a girl.* They'll use wedding bands swinging from thread, tea leaves, tarot, cravings, or any hocus-pocus to predict the baby's sex. (I know a mom-to-be who had a constant craving for sweet red wine, which of course, she could not succumb to. An old woman told her the baby would be red-haired, and that's exactly what she got. It was not a family trait. So who knows?)

Once the baby is born, it doesn't stop. Strangers will look at your kid and say the damndest things. *Your baby's really small for its age . . . your baby's overweight . . . your baby's color isn't good—give it carrot juice.* If you query these advisors, frequently they are not parents! Your hipshot (and justified) response might be, *You're really stupid for your age . . .* but as annoying as these buddinskis are, they are trying to be helpful.

A grand master of dealing with morons was Bob Hope. He had three stock lines that are absolutely meaningless, yet seem to mollify even the most aggressive busybodies. These were Bob's gems:

Isn't that somthin'?

How about that?

And my personal favorite:

Is that so?

Not only are these retorts a foolproof brush-off for meddlesome advice-givers, they are invaluable in side-stepping verbal bait cast by political zealots as well as sundry imbeciles and psychotics. They never realize you've neither agreed nor disagreed, believed or even processed their nonsense, yet they go away without feeling slighted.

This all works quite well with the many mouthy strangers you'll encounter. But what happens if that interfering person is a house-guest? Like, say, your in-laws? Or maybe it's even your own mom. No one is more qualified to rate her child-rearing abilities than you. Are you going to let her monkey with your kid?

Of course, all women, whether or not they are moms, think they know more about babies and children than any man. That's a horse shit, sexist assumption, isn't it? And dig, MACK DADDY— woe unto he who performs any aspect of child care with more élan, speed, or success than a female. To do so is to best her at what she assumes is her genetic calling, and for this she will revile you. Case in point? Aunt Zelda drops by for a visit with her new nephew. She cuddles and plays with him for a while, then puts him down while she phones in an appointment with her hairdresser (her spun-sugar-lacquered bee hive needs shoring up). Soon, baby starts to cry. You reach for her, but Zelda, giving you a look that says "away, silly man," snatches your baby and starts to rock him. But, it isn't working. She tries all her best moves, but the baby continues to wail. What to do? You watch as Zelda grows more agitated—with your baby and especially herself.

Your baby is thinking, *Who is this leather-faced harridan, with breath like buffalo farts and perfume that smells like Daddy's gym bag?*

Best course of action is probably to blame the baby. *He's not accustomed to you, Aunt Zelda, he just misses his daddy.* This will dull her rage, but not extinguish it. In her mind what you've done is tantamount to snatching the Strat from Hendrix and laying down some *Purple Haze* riffs he hadn't thought of.

Then there are the professional oracles, authoritative because of their "credentials," and ubiquitous with books, TV, and radio shows and the legions of fans that feed their media empires. Who's to say whether they know what they're talking about? Can you really trust diet advice from that guy with the 40-inch waistline?

Up until the 1960s, there were dozens of M.D.s who endorsed various brands of cigarettes as being *healthful* and *beneficial to nerves and digestion*. Everybody bullshits, whether paid to or not. MACK DADDIES are not rubes. They've got their bullshit filters up and screening everything they hear and see, from the office to the backyard fence.

Here's a good rule of thumb. The less someone tends to use the phrase *I don't know*, the more full of shit he is. Remember, nobody knows your kid like you and mommy. Every kid is different. When it comes to yours, YOU are the experts.

How to Make Your Child Fearless

They say we come into the world with only one fear—the fear of falling. All others are acquired. That's probably true.

FDR was right. *The only thing we have to fear is fear itself*. When reviewing their lives, most people would find fear at the root of their mistakes. And odds are, many of those fears were handed to us by our parents. MACK DADDIES can and must break the cycle of fear.

You can start making your baby fearless from jump. First, do not make him a hot-house plant. Take him outside on a windy day— let him feel it in his face. If it's 30 below, wrap him up and take him out anyway. Give him spirited rides on your knee. If he looks scared, laugh and he'll laugh with you. Carry him around the house on your shoulder—give him a commanding view and let him feel like king shit. Both my daughters loved what I call the football hold. Babies spend way too much time on their backs, so I would hold them around the middle like a football and walk around. They liked it and it gave them a perspective kids who are always in strollers or carried on their backs don't get. Be gentle, but not too gentle. When they weather a little bump or two, they won't be so quick to freak about a more serious shock.

The single most important duty of the MACK DADDY is to

eradicate his kid's fears (and not cultivate any new ones). If you don't, you'll spend your life watching scenes of defeat and mediocrity. Scenes like watching your boy put on the gloom face on his way to school because some pint-size prick is bullying him. Or watching your daughter (who you know damn well has pipes like Celine) stand in the chorus while somebody else's tone-deaf kid is front and center stage belting out "Tomorrow."

If you can eliminate your child's fear, you'll get to revel in his triumphs, accomplishments, and happiness.

Fear is the great robber. It's why we procrastinate. It's what separates rock stars from idiot air guitarists. The dope in the corner office has no fear, while the smart guy in the cubicle is riddled with it.

Helping your child overcome fear goes hand-in-hand with the other MACK DADDY mandate, *helping your child find his or her bliss*. That sounds rather New-Age goofy, but damn, it's so true and vital to not wasting a life. The overwhelming majority of souls spend their lives trudging off to some heinous job just to keep a roof over their head. Yet, who among us doesn't harbor some dream of greatness? Stop any seven-year-old and ask him, *What do you want to be when you grow up?* How many will reply, *I'd like to be a faceless, human drone in a huge, multinational conglomerate, and please may I also feel bored, frustrated, and unfulfilled all the days of my life?*

Most of us *know* what we'd like to be doing. (Of course, there are many who would prefer to just get high, screw off, and let it roll. And that's fine, because we'll always need people to do menial tasks for menial pay.) But somewhere along the line, we lose sight of our bliss.

Plenty of little boys want to be star athletes. Damn few have what it takes. A MACK DADDY will encourage his kid to chase his dreams, while also helping him to be flexible and realistic in that pursuit. A kid with Michael Jordan aspirations who tops out at five feet seven will *not* likely be drafted by the NBA. But maybe his MACK DADDY steers him toward player management, or coaching, or calling the game or starting a minor-league franchise. He can make a great living and still be a part of what he loves— basketball.

The world is filled with guys who didn't have the hands-on ability to make it in a given field, yet still became wildly successful in that field. Can Donald Trump draw blueprints? Can David Geffen play guitar? Can Don King box? Can Keanu Reeves act? (Rim-shot, please.)

By the time your kid is two or three, his interests may begin to emerge. Does he spend all his time stacking building blocks into I.M. Pei shapes? Or does he constantly pluck at your guitar or piano? Maybe you can't tear him away from the coloring books or his bat and ball. Of course, his interests can and will change. But you've got to be watching and discerning what's merely a fleeting fascination from what really floats his boat. And unlike Der Fuehrer Daddy, be absolutely certain your efforts to help him discover his bliss aren't masking *your* wish fulfillment.

You see it all the time, from Little League fields to putting greens to tennis courts . . . psycho Der Fuehrer Daddies . . . a crazed look in their eyes and veins throbbing in their necks . . . determined to make their kids the next Roger Clemens, Tiger, or Venus. It's hard and sometimes heartbreaking to watch.

When a kid evinces a strong interest in something, MACK DADDIES cultivate it. If the kid wants some piano/ballet/art classes, find the $$. A great place would be in cutting one or two of those pay-TV channels.

Whenever possible, work a pay-by-the-lesson deal with the school. My daughter wanted tap lessons. After two of them, she refused to return. Turns out, she was in it for the *shoes*.

As you help your child find that bliss (it just might be selling insurance like Daddy or Uncle Mort—that's okay, too), work on removing the fear that will hold him back from greatness. As my grandmother said, "Fortune favors the brave."

Cultivating Courage/Banishing Bashfulness

Case in point: as a family, we like to take evening strolls around a nearby lake. One time, Olivia brought her soccer ball. In no time flat, she kicked the thing 20 feet out into the water. I wasn't about to wade in for a $4.99 ball, so we suggested she wait and see if the wind might blow it back to shore. The wind did not cooperate. Every time it seemed to be headed our way, the wind would shift and blow it farther toward the middle. Olivia was frantic. It was getting dark, and I was preparing a "that's how it goes, be more careful with your stuff" speech.

Way in the distance, we saw a flat-bottom boat approaching with a few people aboard enjoying cocktails and a sail. My brilliant wife suggested Olivia ask the boater for help. Like a greyhound, she took off along the shore, her five-year-old legs a blur of motion, until she was near enough to the boat to be heard.

"Excuse me! Excuse me," she called to the boaters. "My ball is stuck in the middle of the lake, would you get it for me?" I could see the rather elderly people in the boat were smitten. They adjusted course, heading for the ball—which, by the way, was quite a detour—as Olivia trotted along the shore, excitedly shouting directions. When they reached the ball, one man opened the side rail, got down on his hands and knees and scooped it from the water. Then they sailed close enough to toss it to me. I handed it to Olivia

At that moment, I felt a tremendous pride in my little girl. She had shown hope, ingenuity, perseverance, moxie, courage, and resolve in one tiny little tableau. I hugged her so close I nearly crushed her. This was a MACK DADDY moment.

The first childhood fear to overcome is bashfulness. Nothing, but nothing, will hold a child, teen, or adult back like shyness. Some parents actually encourage it, thinking it's cute. Maybe so, but it's also a ticket to Palookaville. As they say, ya gotta have elbows.

That's not to say you want your kid to be an obnoxious, grasping boor. But there's a way to make desires known without pissing people off.

One of my favorite flicks is *The Last Detail*. In it, Randy Quaid plays Meadows, a hapless teenaged sailor facing an eight-year prison term for stealing $40. Taking him to prison is Jack Nicholson, an older, wiser gob. En route, they stop in a hamburger joint. Randy orders a cheeseburger, asking Nicholson, "Think they'll melt the cheese on the burgers? I like the cheese melted."

The waiter brings the burger.

"Cheese melted enough for ya?" asks Nicholson.

"Sure."

Nicholson lifts the burger bun.

" 'T aint melted at all."

"It's all right," says the timid Quaid.

"Send the goddamn thing back, Meadows, you're payin' for it."

"It's all right."

"Meadows, have it the way you want it!"

Nicholson summons the waiter and sends it back to have the cheese melted. That brief scene, more than any other I've ever seen on a page or celluloid, illustrates what separates the champ from the chump. Making your child comfortable about voicing his desires is the keystone of success and fulfillment. How to do it? Practice.

Conquering Fear
When you take him out to eat, whether McDonald's or a four-star feed, let him order his own food. When he wants to know where the water fountain/bathroom/Coke machine is . . . do *not* ask for him. Encourage him to approach the security guy/usher/

authority figure and ask for him- or herself. When you buy him shoes and clothing, don't accept a shrugged "it's okay" when asking about fit and comfort.

Praise the shit out of your kids. When they sing a song, applaud. When they tell a joke, laugh. When they draw a picture, hang it over the couch. Then, back up your approval with tangibles. Every kid loves stickers. When my daughter does something exemplary, we thumb a sticker onto a trophy chart on her bedroom door.

It's never too early to start building your kid's ego, and if it's been neglected or suppressed, the damage is very, very hard to repair. Remember, who your kid will be his entire life will be greatly determined by age five.

Don't let him quit, and remember the bromide "a cinch by the inch and hard by the yard." My daughter was not a natural when it came to two-wheeling. So, I began teaching her to ride by increments as small as three feet. It took a hell of a long time, but it worked.

Piss-your-pants funnyman Chris Rock admits, "I wasn't the funniest kid in school. But I worked harder at it than the other guys." And you can bet someone at home laughed his ass off at Chris's schtick—even when it sucked.

Fantasy artist Frank Frazetta, whose talents brought Tarzan and Conan the Barbarian to life, sold his first crayon drawing to his grandma at age three . . . for a penny.

Never mistake caution for fear. Daredevils are not fearless, they're morons. A truly fearless kid will have the balls to stare down a dare and say, "You first, asshole." A kid who is afraid, with a fragile ego, will take the dare and wind up injured, dead, or imprisoned.

Confidence flows from an inner reservoir of self-love. And if your child has it, he or she will be unstoppable. It is absolutely astonishing how many people become hugely successful in endeavors for which they are uniquely *handicapped*. Barbara Walters and Tom Brokaw—broadcasters with obvious speech impediments. Lauren Hutton, '70s supermodel, had a gap-toothed smile that would have stopped anyone else. Yet at her peak it was considered so sexy, models with perfect teeth were paying dentists to drill spaces *into* their smiles.

Speaking of gapped teeth, Arnold Schwarzenegger had one you could drive a Humvee through. With zero acting experience, less than classic looks, and a laughable, punch-line accent, he was the reigning box-office king for years. Then when politics struck his fancy, he upended a statewide political machine and bested cobras that had been in the game when he was still a young gym rat in Austria. But is there any mystery to his success? None whatsoever. Nobody loves Arnold like Arnold, so the world loves him, too. As he told Letterman shortly after marrying Maria Shriver, "I tink ah ahm da best ting evah to hoppen to dah Kennedy fomilee."

Look at successful people in any field, whether business, politics, or entertainment—none is perfect, all have flaws. But their egos are without crack or blemish and therefore they prevail.

Chapter 6

1–3 Years

"Daddy, I have to Make Pee-pee!"

With kids, nature doesn't call, it shouts. And when your kid complains of a full bladder, you've got maybe 60 seconds. What to do?

MACK DADDY *Outdoor* Protocol

The secret street leak. You did it in college. Make it a family tradition.

Toddlers are short and easy to conceal. Take a look around. How about next to that dumpster? Behind that tree. Behind the car door. If somebody spots you, so what? It's a *baby*! Chill out, Mr. Civic Watchdog. (In Singapore, this attitude is not an option.)

At the beach and too far to make it to the toilet? Hold up a towel like a windbreak and make sure you're upwind. Did we hear harrumphs from an EPA busybody? What's three ounces of toddler tinkle compared with the tons of gull shit caking that jetty? *Get over there with a wire brush this instant!*

MACK DADDY *Indoor* Protocol

When need arises, you and your child might be anywhere—like a big-box hardware store, where the men's room invariably has piss

106

pooled to rice-paddy depth. And the toilets are backed up to Barstow. How to deal?

Let's see with the other guys are doing.

- Distant Dad: Don't ask him, he's playing golf.
- Lactating Dad: He's got a Hazmat suit that zips out of its own pocket. And a backpack power-washer loaded with bleach.
- Rubber-Stamp Dad: His wife's home *nursing* the four-year-old. He's okay with that.
- Der Fuehrer Dad: He's pre-emptive: "Nobody leaves the house until bladders and bowels are *empty*! On the count of three, you will *void*!"
- MACK DADDY: Here's a technique that helps improve balance and upper body-strength while letting your child whiz.

  For girls: Roll up your trousers a couple of inches. Pick up your child before you go inside. Whisk her into a stall. Shut the door with foot. Kick up the seat with foot. Put her feet on the toilet paper holder. Pull down her pants. Then, one arm under her knees and the other under her arms, hold her above the bowl and don't forget to compensate for trajectory. That means 12 to 18 inches off-center. If you miss a little, so what—your Reeboks are already soaked.

  For boys, same drill, a little easier: Stand him with a leg on either side of the rim and let fly. For added fun, throw in a target so he can work on his aim. (Memo to men's room designers: Why do the stall doors always open *IN*, you morons!?) When finished, reverse the sequence. If properly done, neither one of you will have touched one filthy, bacteria-covered surface in the shithouse. As Martha says, that's a *good* thing.

When entering a plane or movie theater, it's always a good idea to scope the exits. When out with the baby, do the same for bathrooms.

What to do when it's number two? Usually, even a kid can forestall a dump until you find a place that's sufficiently sanitary. Once you do, cover that seat with layers of paper. When finished, scrub his/her mitts. Keep a package of baby wipes in the glove box or pocket. They're great for disinfecting little hands.

A few words about genital nomenclature. Part of a child's beauty is its innocence. Do you really want to hear your child talk like Nancy Friday? Why use anus, penis, and vagina? What purpose does that serve? What's wrong with baby names for baby parts?

It could save you legal hassles. When my daughter was about three, I had some difficulty getting her situated in the shopping cart at a crowded supermarket. As she plopped into the seat, she loudly scolded, "Daddy, don't bang my wee-woe!" Good thing we called her vagina a wee-woe.

You Cannot Train a Toilet

Like the old saw goes, you can lead a horse to water, but you can't make him drink. It's pretty much the same with kids and toilets. There are dozens of theories on how to get a kid to use toilets, but ultimately when he's ready, he will.

Kids are kooky about it. Some seem ready when they're just a year or so old and may actually use it regularly. Then one day, bam, it's like someone erased their hard drive and it's back to diapers.

Some people buy little kiddy dumpers. (I've seen them in kitchens—yeccch.) Sometimes they're found in the bathroom next to the kitty litter box, another pleasant, aromatic device. Seems like a separate toilet just complicates things. Why not just opt for a little baby toilet seat that fits right on the grown-up toilet? That way, there's no "outgrowing" a baby toilet.

As with most things, a routine will be best. Try to sit him on the commode at the same time each day for the same duration. If it doesn't happen, don't chain him to it. You just can't force these things—and you don't want the kid to associate the toilet with misery.

Some kids like complete privacy. Others want to be kept company, told stories, or sing songs with you. You can also invent stories—a good one is that fish eat poo poo and it's feeding time. (Don't be surprised if later in life your child reviles seafood.)

They make all kinds of training pants/diapers. It's important to put the kid in clothes he can shuck instantly—no tricky belt buckles or drawstrings to fool with.

Some kids are ultra-independent and insist on wiping themselves. That's okay, but they'll usually do a lousy job, so it's time for more Jedi mind tricks. Ask if he'll teach you how to do it so good and you can compensate for his mistakes. By the way, *never* throw a baby wipe in the can. They will clog your pipes for certain.

Some kids don't like to flush. Maybe they're afraid of the noise. You can get them past that by throwing bits of paper in and having a race to see whose disappears first.

Some people actually get competitive with this stuff—you know, *My little Montague is only eleven months and not only is he toilet trained, once he finishes up his business, he puts fresh potpourri in the bowl on the vanity.* Don't play that game. How early or late a kid is toilet trained has no more bearing on his intelligence or development than whether he prefers vanilla or strawberry.

If They Call You an Animal, Be Flattered

- Daddy catfish starves himself for several weeks while he carries the eggs of his young in his mouth. Only when they're ready to hatch does he finally off-load and grab some cheese puffs and a beer.
- Marmoset monkeys take the babies from birth and only bring them to Mommy for nipple snacks. He teaches it to eat solid food. Damned accommodating, no?
- A daddy Emperor penguin keeps his eggs on his feet, covered by a flap of feathers. This goes on for 60 days,

during which time he eats not a morsel. These guys lose about 25 pounds (a third of their body weight) during the ordeal.

- Rheas are South American ostriches. Once their baby is hatched, pop does *everything* until they can survive solo. (Where the *hell* is mom?)
- There's a bird in the baking Kalahari called a Sand Grouse. When water is unavailable (like, always) he'll fly 50 miles to a source, soak himself, and fly back so his chicks can drink from his water-logged feathers.
- It's odd that male wolves are synonymous with womanizers. In fact, the opposite is true. When Mommy has pups, he brings home the groceries, defends the den from raiders, and teaches his pups to survive.
- Even the odious cockroach has an endearing quality. His offspring require heavy doses of nitrogen, so papa roach travels miles to load up on nitrogen-rich avian shit. Then he trucks it back to the hungry hatchlings for a bird turd buffet. Disgusting, but valiant.

It's Not a Bathtub—It's SpongeBob's Neighborhood

The frequency of baby baths depends on a bunch of things. How often your baby dumps and pees. The consistency of the dumps. The way you diaper him. How he's built.

Girls need more bathing than boys because their internal plumbing is susceptible to many problems. When she takes a mostly liquid dump, some will get into her vagina, and that's not good. Can you get it all out with a baby wipe? Maybe, but why risk it? Plunk her in the bath and be sure.

For the first few months, the best (and most fun) place to bathe the baby is in the kitchen sink. They make these cool little plastic tubs, with a partition at the knees for fresh rinse water. You don't need baby shampoo—there are several brands of complete baby body wash that won't sting their eyes. The first or second bath may scare hell out of her, but if you do it right, you can turn her into a water-lovin' little mermaid.

Temperature is key. When she's soaped up, she'll be slick and hard to hold on to. Get a plastic cup for the rinse—you don't need any glass around. Make sure the towel is close by *before* you start. If you use a nice temperature and don't drop her, and smile a lot, she'll come to enjoy it.

The after-bath drill is equally important. You don't like to stand wet in a cold draft, neither do kids. Wrap her in a towel the second she exits that bath.

A full rinse is also key. Especially in the butt crack and crotch. Any soap residue will soon itch like hell and you'll have a screaming mimi on your hands.

If your kid is a plumper, here's a couple of tips. Those baby thunder thighs produce deep fat folds that will get funky and raw if not aired out. If your baby's a chunk, let him go butt naked for a few hours a day so the air can circulate. When you change diapers, pull those fat folds apart and see what's going on in there. If it's damp, get the hair dryer, put it on its coolest setting, and dry him out.

When your baby's been fed, slept, and still cries, check the butt crack and groin area. Often there's an itch that's driving him crazy.

By three to five months, the sink tub will get a little cramped. By now their spines are stiffening, and you can buy a little bath chair and bathe him in the tub. When you rinse the head, try to keep it upright so water doesn't flow into his ears. Of course, never walk away, even for a second.

Sometimes with my older daughter I'm running on fumes by bath time and we have to do it commando style. (For more on *commando-style,* see "Running Errands," later in this chapter.) But if there's time, I let her get a good soak, submerge her Barbie dolls (rubber ducks and bath toys don't interest her, just dunking three Barbie dolls. Looks like a stop-action animation set for Cypress Gardens) and play SpongeBob's neighborhood. This pretend tradition began one night when she was overtired and didn't want a bath. She was giving me a tough time. Then I had a eureka moment. There was a pineapple in the fridge. I grabbed it and threw it into the tub.

"Look, Olivia, it's SpongeBob's house!" She was in that tub pronto. No more tears, no more fights. Until it was time to get her *out* of the tub. Then I came up with some other diversionary tactic nonsense.

Women really have an edge on men in this department. Hard-wired in the art of deception, they just know how to wheedle, tease, manipulate, lie, and redirect. Think of how easily you've been finessed by women—a kid is even less of a challenge. Watch savvy moms with their kids. Learn and copy.

My daughter has the thickest, most luxurious hair imaginable. After a shampoo, the knots are impossible. We tried all kinds of conditioners—they just made the knots feel silky. The only one that worked was called Infusium23.

The after-bath comb-out is a good coda to the process of calming a wired kid and getting her ready to sleep. I always enjoy it. Olivia sits on my lap and babbles about everything. By the time I'm finished, her eyes look heavy and she's almost asleep. I'm dreading the day she tells me she wants to do it herself. Another MACK DADDY perk will be gone forever.

Laundering Your Language

All of your adult life, you've been able to unleash torrents of profanity at cretinous motorists, televised politicos, and Rosie O'Donnell. Then one day, a 21-pound censor who can barely form words herself forces you to clean up your potty mouth.

(MACK DADDY aside: There is absolutely nothing wrong with profanity, foul language, cursing. It's merely a matter of where and at or in front of whom. People who do not curse, and claim they never do, are either liars or psychotics. Never, ever trust anyone who claims a pure mouth. They are invariably deceitful, vicious little shits.)

Here's how my filth-flaming days dwindled. We like to eat dinner on the patio and be one with nature. In late summer, blooming hedges bring swarms of yellow jackets. (MACK DADDY tip: keep the ketchup or tomato sauce far away—that's usually what the pointy-assed little bastards are after.) On this particular evening, they really got annoying and I began to flail at them with a fly swatter. I'd punctuate every missed swing with "Fuck!"

Olivia wasn't really talking yet, just mumbling Mama and Da-da. Irene told me to "knock it off, your daughter is listening."

"Are you nuts? She's 14 months old. It doesn't matter what I say in front of her. Maybe in a year it will."

Irene drilled me with her patented *you'll eat those words, nitwit* stare. I continued flailing and swearing.

Same time, same place, 24 hours later. I'm prepping the grill for a feed and from behind I hear Olivia's tiny voice . . . *Fuck! Fuck! Fuck!* I turn to see her, flyswatter in hand, whipping on yellow jackets just as I had the previous night.

There wasn't much said over that dinner, and I realized the error of my ways.

So, how do you clean up your language? Think of it more as *where*. The toughest venue will be the car—the sanctum sanctorum of the American male, where you've had sexual Olympiads, slept off binge drinking, screamed with Sammy Hagar, and most important, bellowed invectives at those ignorant shitheads in cell phone trances.

The kid's in the backseat and you just forget she's there. Some pinhead cuts you off and you let the syllables fly.

ps . . . Will you explain to her the meaning and syntax of
_ucksuckingshitforbrainsasshole in the car or wait until
you get home so she can ask Mommy? Another conundrum.

Try substituting growls and roars. Or, double up on the poker
night or boys' night out, when men can talk like men and not
have to edit one cathartic, explosive consonant. Colorful language
is a gift from God and has its place.

Let's see how those other guys handle the language problem.

- Lactating Daddy: Only uses gosh, golly and darn, but now his
  WWP (that's Wife With Penis) insists he say them without so
  much *hate*.

- Rubber-Stamp Daddy: He asks his wife's permission to get
  angry.

- Der Fuehrer Daddy: No problem. He curses in Low German.

- Daddy Distant: Does not curse. Has been so brainwashed by
  corporate Sensitivity Training Sessions that he now thanks
  assholes for their rude behavior.

The Choice Scam

What do tots want? Independence. They want to run the show.
When a cranky four-year-old doesn't want to go to bed/eat
dinner/brush his teeth/whatever—he finds it so easy and
rebelliously satisfying to shout *NO!* Feels great, doesn't it? *No* is
empowering. When that imbecile telemarketer calls just as you
are about to sink your teeth into a porterhouse, doesn't it feel
great to say "no"? Your kid gets the same thrill from nixing your
requests.

Here's a cool Jedi mind trick that will help curtail the shouting
matches: offer a *perceived* choice. Slick marketers know how
perceived choice gives softheaded consumers the illusion of
control. *How do you want your latte? Decaf, no-fat, 2 percent, or*

whole milk? Will that SUV be the XL Deluxe Alpine Adventurer or the Captain Corsair Signature Road Clipper? Coffee is coffee and a truck is a truck and as you sit powerless in grid-locked traffic on your way to an office filled with people you truly wish would *die,* slipping that custom cup of crank into the capstan-evocative cup holder does give you a soupcon of sovereignty.

Your kid feels the same way. You control every aspect of his life and godammit, he's had enough! So when you're heading for nursery school on a sub-zero morning and he's in a barefoot, Lilo & Stitch frame of mind, instead of roaring "Put your shoes on now," try: "Titus . . . would you rather wear your Official NASA Galactic Explorers with the shock-proof arch, or your new BLING-BOY rhinestone pave saddle shoes?"

First, this will divert his attention from his primary goal, which is breaking your balls. Second, it negates the whole barefoot issue and makes his shod feet fait accompli. Third, it taxes his little mind, forcing a decision. Somewhere in that mental morass, he'll get a visceral feeling that he's calling the shots. Before you know it, he's at school wearing shoes and you're in gridlock sipping a latte in your *Master and Commander* motif truck. With the exertion you saved by not battling Titus, you'll have more energy to do your job/go postal/behead your boss. That's a win-win deal, for everyone, eh?

MACK DADDY Aside

A long time ago, I was staying with my cousins. They had five kids—the eldest daughter was about 13 or 14 and a precocious, glib wise-ass. The younger four had already left for school on a bitter cold morning. The teen daughter was going through some kind of Kung Fu Chick-Monk phase, and wanted to wear flip-flops instead of shoes—out into the slush. Her mom gave her the expected litany of reasons why not—pneumonia, chilblains, rheumatic fever, cuts and abrasions, but the little bitch wouldn't budge. Finally, her mom lost it, shrieking, "Put . . . on . . . your . . . fucking . . . shoes!"

There was a four-second silence. Then, looking at a pile of shoes by the door, the daughter enquired, "Which ones are my *fucking* shoes?"

Running Errands Without Your Kid Running You

Infants can be a snap. Some sleep all the time, go wherever the hell you say when you say, and drink the same boring goop day in day out for months. Need to hit the supermarket? Just snap that car seat into the base and go. If the baby does gripe, choose from this simple menu of three reasons: hunger, full diaper, fatigue. You can feed or change them anywhere, and if you can lay them sorta flat, they'll sleep damn near anywhere, too. They don't care about the decor, or that you've blown past Captain Crunch without saluting or that you haven't stocked up on SpongeBob Band-Aids.

By the time your baby can talk, she'll have her own agenda, and woe unto you if it differs from hers. Time for some psychological judo.

When you need to hit the supermarket and your tot gives you static, choose from an even simpler menu of two reasons: fatigue and boredom. Fatigue is tougher to deal with, because by this age, they need more room to conk out, and visual and aural stimuli will prevent sleep. Always try to time your errand running with a reasonably well-slept kid. When he's tired, you'll be dealing with an irrational psychopath. (See more about this in "Tantrums".)

Boredom is the second biggest reason for whining, complaining, and non-cooperation. But, if you're a crafty MACK DADDY, you can finesse your kid. Think about it—would you enjoy sitting in a wire cart, being pushed around a big, fluorescent-lit place while your old man tries to mentally calculate whether the Big Buy

12-roll package of Scott asswipe is really a better deal than three four-packs? Hell no. You'd kick and scream and try to stiff-arm a pyramid of Classico Fire-roasted Tomato sauce, too.

Here's a Jedi mind trick I borrowed from my genius wife. Before you leave the house (or in the car), tell your little darling that you're going to the supermarket and you need her help. Tell her there are some things on your list—beer, tortillas, peanut-butter-filled pretzel nuggets, T-bone steaks—that's the daddy/man list. You need her help with the mommy/girl list. You can go through the theater of writing it with her, or grab that losing Lotto ticket from your wallet—just give her something to hold and look at and pretend to read and *involve* her. That is the magic word—*involve*.

As you strafe the aisles, ask her opinion on the Big Buy 12-roll deal. You'll get some fun answers.

In the parking lot, run as you push her in the cart. Kids love that, and it makes a nice reward for good behavior.

By the time my daughter was four, she was enough of a girly-girl to know she abhorred my temple of do-it-yourself pleasures, Home Depot. But when I needed plywood, or a pipe snake, or some Corry's Slug & Snail Death on a Saturday morning, I couldn't leave her home alone.

"I hate that stupid place with all that stupid boy stuff! Why don't they sell dresses?" she bitched.

And I thought, *Yeah . . . Vera Wang's missing a helluva distribution channel.*

Then, an idea. My daughter is a flower freak. Loves them.

"Sweetheart, I know you hate Home Depot. But they have girl stuff there, too."

Her face brightened. "Like what?"

As we drove over, I threw another Jedi mind trick at her. I *stated the agenda.* Some kids are "go-with-the-flow"—not Olivia. A total control freak, she *must* know the agenda: if there are deviations, they better be good.

"First, I need to get my boy-stuff *commando-style.*" That's another MACK DADDY precept. Get the kid accustomed to doing certain things *commando style.* These are tasks, which, when time is available, may be lingered over. But if time is short, they must go like shit through a goose. Some of our typical commando-style endeavors are baths, grocery shopping, dressing, and hand washing. Once you get them accustomed to commando-style activities, they don't get pissed off about being rushed. In fact, sometimes you can get them to help you beat the clock.

"Then, once I get all that stuff, we can look at the flowers and see if there are any ones for us." Notice, I didn't tell her we were *buying* flowers—that would constitute bribing her for her cooperation—a last-resort option.

We got to Home Depot, I got all the crap I needed and then we headed to the nursery. Olivia scoped out all the blooms. We finally found a plant that worked for the front yard. But if we hadn't, there would have been no purchase, and she would have been cool with it because she got the agenda *in advance.*

Tantrums

Some time ago, I recall being in a supermarket where a young mom pushed a tot in the cart. She was a pretty typical three-year-old, with pigtails and freckles. And she was having a seismic shit-fit in hi-def Technicolor. Her arms pumped, her legs kicked, she knocked goods off the shelves, she grabbed the sides and rocked the cart so hard I thought it would tip over. She screamed blood-curdling, crystal-shattering screams. Heads turned, people stopped, people stared.

Through the entire scene, her mom paid her no more attention than she would a head of lettuce. Not only was she unfazed, her face bore a beatific expression of rapture. It seemed the kid never took a breath. The storm raged as Mommy calmly walked the aisles, shopping list in hand, filling her cart.

At the checkout, the performance continued at full volume. Mommy paid the clerk, smiled sweetly, and mouthed "thank you." (No words could be heard—this kid could have drowned out the turbines on a C-5 Galaxy.)

She pushed the cart out to the street and unloaded her groceries into the trunk of her VW bug. (There was a daisy in the dashboard vase.) She opened the passenger door and the girl got in and stood on the passenger seat. Then Mommy got behind the wheel. The kid was still screaming and flailing. Mommy checked her hair and makeup in the rearview. Then, she stiff-armed her daughter, flipping her right over the seat and into the rear. As she drove away, I could see the kid's sneakers up by the headrest.

When a toddler wigs out, it's usually not for the reason he states. Rarely is it about the fact that you didn't let him augment his pirate costume with the 12-inch carving knife, or a wheel fell off his trike. The underlying cause of most tantrums is fatigue. Kids need their sleep like they need air. Problem is, they don't always know when they're tired. If you can regulate their sleep and be sure they get sufficient amounts when they need it, you'll rarely have to employ a straitjacket and Thorazine drip.

Every schedule goes sideways now and then, and that's when you'll need body armor. Kids in tantrums are like psychotics on PCP. They just don't care. You can't reason with them. They'll scream too loud for you to be heard.

The crazy, serene bitch in the supermarket was actually handling it very well, until she flipped the kid. The very worst thing you can do is get pissed off too and start yelling. This will only escalate the volume and lengthen the duration.

You can stand there and watch, but be sure he's not about to put his head through a pane of glass or body-roll into traffic. You can try to speak softly to him—the words are irrelevant—it's just for the calming effect of your voice. Sometimes a slow hug can end a tantrum.

The older the kid, the tougher it is to deal. If she throws the tantrum on foot, this can be very dangerous—with her mind in the insanity zone and her vision blurred by tears, she could run into anything. If that's the situation, you must restrain her. Pick her up off the ground and hold her while she flails, if necessary.

Once the tantrum passes, don't bother trying to get an explanation—it's unlikely the kid will remember what lit her fuse. Don't look for an apology, either. Just get past it. Help her pick up the toys she flung around the room or repair whatever damages she caused. Somewhere in her little head, she knows she was a jerk and she's embarrassed.

You know damn well that when no one's around, you throw 'em, too.

Sibling Rivalry

Think about it—there you are—only child, center of Mommy and Daddy's universe, and nearly the same status with Grandma and Grandpa, the grocer, the neighbors. Your every word, expression, and fart is considered brilliant, funny, and sweetly aromatic. Then one day Mommy's belly swells. You are told there is *another*. Would you welcome a younger brother or sister?

Kids can be insanely jealous. When my daughter was about three, I attended a kiddie party at one of her friend's homes. When the music started, a tiny little girl I didn't know took my hands and began to dance with me. Suddenly, I heard a shrieked "*Noooooooo!*" and Olivia leapt between us, like Mills Lane separating two middleweights in a clinch. I was astonished at the ferocity of her outrage.

Head off those fraternal resentments from the start. Best way is to give all the visual cues that firstborn is still king shit. When the new baby arrives, make sure Daddy (and *no one else*) takes the older child to see Mommy at the hospital. When you enter her room, be sure Mommy is not holding the baby. Have a present from the new baby to the older child and vice versa. Let the older child hold the baby first, then bring it to Mommy. Yeah, it sounds like some kooky, other-hemisphere etiquette, but we are all hardwired with instinctive protocols and a misstep can ignite deep resentments.

If they're going to share a bedroom, you have to lay a lot of groundwork in advance. Long before the baby is born, talk up the thrill it will be to have company at night. That she'll get to be a big sister and help take care of the baby just like a grown-up girl. Involve her by asking her to donate some of her old stuffed toys to the new one. Give her choices—*When baby sister comes home, do you think her crib should go here or here?* In our case, there was no real choice. I just rolled it a few inches side to side and asked her opinion. *On which side of it should we put the Diaper Genie?* Get her into a magnanimous state of mind. If you saved all the para- phernalia from the first baby, make a big deal out of the older kid "donating" his kiddie bathtub, bottles, sippy cups, and so on.

After you've done all the advance work, the real tough part comes. That baby is new, and it's going to need and get more attention than her older sibling. MACK DADDY's job is to equally distribute attention.

When the baby amazes you by finally gripping a bottle in his hands, check the face of your older child, because he's thinking, *big deal. Daddy's flipping over a stupid bottle when five minutes ago I counted to a hundred?* Then tell him—*you held a bottle just like that—baby must be copying you!*

Lots of baby gifts will arrive. People with kids usually slip something in for the older kid. If unsure of the contents, stash it somewhere until your older kid isn't present. Why make her feel unloved?

Beware of strangers. When you're out with an infant, your older child becomes invisible. You run into people who stop and smile and make a fuss over the baby, and suddenly your older baby feels like an untouchable. My fix-it is this—as soon as they approach the baby, I scoop Olivia up and say, "And here's my number ONE girl, Olivia. Isn't she beautiful too?" People catch on fast and lavish her with compliments.

You tell white lies every day, all day. They are society's lubricant. *Hey boss, great idea! Slick lookin' Hyundai, Joe! Nice hat, Tiffany!* Why not afford your older kid the same feel-good compliments? As the novelty of a younger sibling waned, my older daughter's resentment toward her increased. Taking a page from government agencies and corporate PR departments, I began to issue *disinformation. Yes Olivia, you are my favorite five-year-old daughter. Of course I love you the most—I've had five years to fall in love with you. Of course you're more beautiful than the baby.* What's the harm? By the time the baby's old enough to know what I'm saying, Olivia won't care anymore.

Once that younger sibling is born, be vigilant to ensure the elder kid is getting the level of attention to which she's grown accustomed. One way is to heavy-up at dinner time. When the baby's at the table, she's going to siphon attention like a black hole, leaving the older one feeling like wallpaper. Solution: occasionally get the baby asleep earlier or delay dinner until she's sleeping so you can lavish attention on the older one—just like the good old days. It works great.

Night Owl Toddlers

Once you get the book on a baby, it's pretty easy to get him to sleep. Toddlers, however, can be much more difficult. And getting that toddler to sleep on time has big benefits for everyone. You and Mom get some time alone. And the next day, a well-slept tot is an easy tot. A sleepy one will be a walking hate crime.

One of the biggest culprits is a dose of TV prior to bed.

Something about it tends to make kids wired, so turn it off at least an hour before bedtime. Ditto any other electronic devices—no PlayStation, Nintendo, MP3s, computer usage, and so on.

No chemical stimulation. That includes caffeine colas with dinner (actually, anything caffeinated for a kid is a lousy idea) and any sweet desserts—especially chocolate. Between the caffeine and sugar, your kid might be up for a month.

Establish a routine of behaviors that signify day is done and the sandman awaits. Pee pee, wash hands, brush teeth, pajamas, read a story, goodnight cuddle, lights out.

As an infant, my first daughter slept like a mummy. Anywhere, anytime. But by the time she was around three years old, bedtime became problematic. So we started the bedtime routine. Trouble is, a kid's entire schedule needs to be well regimented throughout the day. And when one segment of it is moved or eliminated, it throws him off-kilter. So if you're on the road and lunch is off by 90 minutes and the afternoon nap never happens, you're probably in for a rough night.

If the tot is really manic, a warm bath with dimmed lights can help. Warm milk, too. Pick a really dull bedtime story and read it like a hypnotist. Make sure the room temp and blankets are just right. Some kids are heat balls, some sleep like hypothermic victims. You just have to experiment. Too warm or cold will keep anybody awake.

Once you have the tot tucked in, make sure you don't ruin all your hard work by cranking the blender for some margaritas. Unless you have beaucoup square footage, you'll probably have to tip toe around until she's in REM cycle.

It's all worth it. When you look in on her and see that angel face snoozing, it will be tough not to grab her and kiss her.

When they get a little older, they can be downright sneaky. More than once, Olivia has feigned sleep. I found out the following day that she had belly-crawled out of bed and from behind the couch, watched most of *Child's Play* with Chucky stabbing, slashing, and calling people *cunts*. Oh great. So now, if we're not watching A&E, we shut her door and leave on the baby monitor.

Why the Library Is a Cool Place

There's one in just about every town. And they're not just about books anymore. Lots of libraries have computers, Internet connections and, instead of handing over your hard-earned cash to some huge video chain for *Cinderella*, it's probably available at the library on tape or DVD.

My wife discovered a library nearby that's fabulous. It's modern, spacious, staffed by really helpful people and has a terrific collection of kid books, videos, DVDs, and music on CD.

Every so often, I'll swing by with my daughter just to have a look. She strafes the kiddie aisles (designed by some smart guy who puts all the shelves at eye level for little ones) and grabs a stackful. I get what I want, and we sit together and expand our minds for a while. Before she could read, I would start her off by reading a couple of stories to her. Then, she'd thumb through picture books for a while, giving me the chance to glance at a few volumes. Now, she's practically on auto pilot. She loves to read and if she comes across something that stumps her, I'm there to help.

Plenty of libraries are offering specialties for kids that are sensational. Many have readings from big name kid authors, magic, storytelling hours, crafts, puppets—all fabulous alternatives to parking them in front of the tube.

Many have online access—you can find out what's available for borrowing and reserve it if it isn't.

Books Your Kid Will Love

Want to raise a maladjusted stooge? It's easy. Just plop a kid in front of the tube and in no time at all, his brain will liquify. Will better content—educational stuff—Baby Einstein and CTW, circumvent brain emulsification? Well, they may not be harmful, but they in NO WAY equal or replace the value of *reading* to a child. Reading to your kid may be the ultimate quality time.

The older the child, the more important the content becomes. For a kid just out of infancy, it's pretty much just words and pictures and close time with Daddy. But as their comprehension grows, what you read to them is critically important. What will you choose?

What do pop divas, TV and movie stars, politicians, and athletes do when their careers droop like a Viagra-deprived satyr? They write children's books. Why do they always choose to write *children's* books? Maybe it's because *you only have to write a few dozen words*, and shazam . . . you're an *author*.

How about Dr. Seuss? They're okay, once in a while. But think of Theordor Geisel's works as more of a side dish than a staple. Wanna light the booster rockets on your kid's imagination? Go for the classics. For young toddlers, that means *The Little Engine That Could. The Little Red Hen. Beatrix Potter. Goodnight Moon.* At the very least, these books are entertaining and educational, without being *pedantic*. At their best, they give a kid something far, far more valuable than knowledge . . . *wisdom*.

Many people make no distinction between wisdom and information. The difference is vast.

Our educational system is predicated on information. Those who can store the greatest quantity and retrieve it on demand excel in school and are deemed smart. But given that definition, a computer with a mediocre hard drive and processor is smarter than the greatest scholar, because its information storage/

retrieval capacity dwarfs any human's. What does all this have to do with the books you read to your kid? Everything.

Will you be sharing an epiphany when you read your kid *Budgie the Little Helicopter* by HRH the (former) Duchess of York, aka, Sarah Ferguson/Weight Watchers commercial pitchwoman?

And what about Madonna? Why did she decide to pen kiddie books? Says the material girl cum Kabbalist, "I'm starting to read to my son. But I couldn't believe how vapid and vacant and empty all the stories were. There's, like, no lessons . . . there's like, no books about anything." Hey Miss Ciccone, like, read, like, on like, below, 'kay?

The works of Hans Christian Andersen, The Brothers Grimm, and Aesop can imbue a tot with the wisdom of Solomon. There's a reason these stories have survived for ages—they don't just entertain kids, they wise them up—without robbing them of their innocence.

Lactating Daddies decry classic kid stories and fairy tales because of their frightening and violent content. But guess what, girly-men? It's a frightening and violent world out there. Fate is fickle—you may not be around to protect your kids. Your un-detected aneurysm could pop like a nuked egg and then where are you?

Shrinks agree that a child's personality and attitude is pretty well formed by age five. If you croak tomorrow, how will your kid fare if his formative thinking has been shaped by the collective scribblings of Madonna, Jane Seymour, and a defunct duchess?

Shit happens. *Especially* to children. Is *Hansel and Gretel* based on fact or fiction? Let's see . . . Do mommies sometimes die young? Do widowed daddies ever marry raging bitches that would prefer their stepchildren dead? Do strangers (witches) ever kidnap and murder kids?

Of course, this cautionary tale is couched in some whimsy, like gingerbread houses and water-taxi/swans, making it palatable to kids. But the lessons contained are rooted in a bedrock of undeniable truths. Someday your parents *will* die. There *are* human monsters that perpetrate unspeakable atrocities on children. Keep your wits about you and be smarter than to leave a trail of friggin' breadcrumbs in the forest.

Aesop, the wisest Greek by far, cut to the chase with his fables. Every last one of them has a chunk of wisdom that will help a kid get through life. And, yes, the classic kiddie stories push some moralistic agendas that our colossally twisted, 21st-century society could use—precepts like fidelity, courage, hard work, thrift, loyalty, responsibility, perseverance, forgiveness, and belief in God—the Ultimate MACK DADDY.

Some "experts" claim little girls who read *Cinderella* and *Beauty and the Beast* are more likely to become victims of violence.

My elder daughter is crazy about all the princess stories. I've read them with her dozens of times. No question about it, Snow White is one *stupid* chick. But some of the others are pretty smart, courageous, and strong. Ultimately, that's the beauty of reading to your child. If you don't agree with the content, you can edit as you go.

How to Read to the Little Doll

Turn off all extraneous lights. If there's noise from the next room, close the door.

There are a few gears you can shift through, depending on the purpose of the reading. With younger kids, the bedtime story is a verbal sleeping pill. So you pick something innocuous, maybe a little boring and read with a hypnotist's delivery.

At other times, you'll want to really set fire to the story. Have you ever wanted to be Eddie Murphy, Chris Rock, or George Carlin? Now's your chance. You can do all the voices, faces, accents, and sound effects you haven't tried since fifth grade. And best of all, your kid will love them. You won't be criticized or rated, just loved.

When you read, use your fingers and point to objects in the illustrations. Encourage the kid to ask you questions—make storytime a dialogue, not a monologue. Ask if he understands what you've read. He'll probably say yes. Then ask a specific question and you may find out he was clueless. Kids have egos, too, and will lie to protect them.

Explain to him the subtleties of the story. When you need to, edit. Some stories will have superfluous text or text written above your kid's level of understanding—don't be afraid to skip over it. You can always go back and read it to him when he's ready. And don't worry about repetition. You'll be bored senseless as you do your 217th reading of the Stinky Easter Egg, but your kid won't.

Change up story time by telling him a story instead of reading one. My kid always says, "Tell me a story about when you were a little boy." There's a terrific way to stretch your imagination while entertaining your child and maybe passing on a little family history. Try to give it a beginning, a middle, and an end. Kids love to imagine you as a kid—isn't that what happens when you play with them?

Here's another variation: once in a while, ask your kid to tell you a story. You can't just let her free-wheel, or she'll get stuck. So if you give a little direction, like, "Tell me about when you won the limbo contest," and then prompt with more questions like, "How did you feel when that happened," or "What was that like," you'll get some interesting yarns and learn more about your child.

Chapter 7

3-6 Years

It's Chow Time

As you'll find with the entire MACK DADDY experience, raising your kid becomes more complex the older he gets. At birth, Mommy's nipple or a warm bottle of formula will be just fine. After a few months, a spoonful of strained bananas. By the time he's ready to eat what you eat, he may have developed some peculiar tastes.

My daughter swung through phases. Early on, she would eat anything. We always encouraged this. Her consumption of fruits and vegetables has always been astonishing. She actually prefers a bowl of strawberries to ice cream.

But by age four or so, it seemed she'd lost some of her sense of gustatory adventure and began demanding hamburgers and refusing new dishes. Where did this come from?

I suspect much of it is learned from other kids. At school, little Madison wrinkles her nose at your kid's asparagus stalk and suddenly asparagus is no good. Some of it is also about texture, and then, some things just do taste lousy. *Lima beans, anyone?*

A MACK DADDY wants to beware of catering to his kid's tastes. I've seen several parents actually offer an array of different dinners to please the picky palates of their kids. If they have the time (or a live-in chef) to indulge such nonsense, great. But basically, everybody should eat the same grub.

My wife has a few creative ways of getting my daughter to eat the right stuff. If she's not eating the tomatoes, my wife talks in the voice of the tomato about how glad we are that the big monster isn't going to eat us. When Olivia bites one, the tomato shrieks and cries for help. Sometimes arranging the veggies on the plate in the shape of a big smiley face helps.

Nutrition aside, there's a far more important aspect of meals, and one meal in particular.

Question:

What simple, ancient ritual that binds families together has become a casualty of our urban, twenty-first century "lifestyle?"

Answer:

Dinner.

The family dinner gets preempted by late nights at the office, traffic, soccer practice, homework, instant messages, and television.

On endless nights in countless homes, greasy paper sacks snatched from drive-thru windows are plopped on kitchen tables, where Mom, Dad, and the kids tear into high-calorie, low-nutrition gunk and skulk off to their respective chambers.

On those rare occasions when the entire family does gather at the dinner table, conversation is frequently nullified by blaring televisions, MP3 players, or eat-and-run participants.

Who can alter this dysfunctional tide and light the path back to the civilized family dinner, where food, conversation and love prevail? You, baby.

The time to set the precedent is the very *first* time you and Mommy and Baby sit down to break bread together. Because by the time that kid's a teenager, it will be too late. If he's Robo-tripping at school you'll no longer be hip enough to know about it.

You know those government ads urging parents to *Talk to your kids* and *Parents: the anti-drug?* Nice sentiment, Uncle Sam, but the question is, *when?* The MACK DADDY answer is at the dinner table, which is reserved for only two things: eating and talking.

Don't even have a TV within eye or earshot of the table. If you like to masticate to music, keep the volume low. This is precious time. This is quality time—family hour. Share it with no one but your wife and kids. Don't answer the telephone—it's probably some gink trying to sell you thermal windows.

In a few years, you want your child accustomed to telling you how his day at school was, or explaining where he got that shiner or who his new best friend is.

Starting the meal with grace or some kind of prayer ain't a bad idea. If that's not your style, do or say something that focuses everyone's attention and clearly sets a tone that *this is a special time each day when we are together and nothing interferes with that.*

Around age three or four, they want to finish up after three bites and go play. "Just say no," to that. Everybody sits down together and nobody leaves until everyone is finished eating.

Here's an etched-in-granite MACK DADDY precept: no controversy at the dinner table—not ever. Whatever subject is raised that causes conflict, hold back until after dinner, and then move to another room. The family dinner needs to be a sanctuary, where everyone can get a break from the hassles of the world and know they are safe from criticism and combat.

Sure it's tough to corral everyone for a sit-down meal. But if you're clever, you can get your crew involved in the dinner prep. Small kids love to be helpful. Let the three-year-old put the napkins on the table or arrange string beans in neat little rows—anything that lets her feel like she's part of the action. When you sit down you can tell her how great her napkins look. When your child's a little older—maybe four or five—have her help make dinner. Kids love pouring ingredients into a pot and stirring it all together. They get a thrill when they feel like they are creating part of the meal.

The same thing works on the back end—enlist their help for clean up—make it a group effort. Have the kids bring the dirty dishes into the kitchen. They can help put utensils in the dishwasher. These tasks may seem meaningless, but they help give kids the idea that being part of a family means helping out and doing chores.

Mackalicious Dining Out

All this kid-centric commercialism is out of control. Bad enough anyone ever has to set foot inside a McDonald's (though founder Ray Kroc is dead, I *still* resent him and his late-riser discriminatory *no breakfast after 11 a.m.* policy), now they block the street view with the *play space*. Several other robot-food purveyors also have play space. They are eyesores that resemble nothing so much as chemical refineries. But hey, isn't just going out to eat a treat in itself—now there has to be play space, too?

Of course, if it's February in Flint, the play space is a godsend. But it's astonishing how often those things are crowded with tykes on warm, sunny days.

Then there's Ronald McDonald, whom market research says is almost as well known as Santa Claus. That may be, kids, but rest assured, that clown isn't giving away *anything*.

Granted, dragging your infant and three-year-old to a four-star restaurant is a waste of money and time. But why always fast food? What's wrong with throwing a few sandwiches in a paper sack, heading for some *real* play space—like a nice, grassy park with fresh air—and calling it a picnic? You'll eat healthier, the kids will play healthier, and you'll save a few bucks.

Those that salivate at the sight of the Golden Arches may wish to inculcate their scions with that gustatory tradition. But for the rest of us, there are alternatives. Why do people have such confidence in the food proffered by the corporate giants? Are the miscreants *they* hire more or less likely to hock a luger into your taco than the family owned and operated joint across the street? I tend to take my chances with the guy whose mortgage payment rides on the quality of his food—not some corporate monolith with a legal department that could fill Michigan Stadium.

Mackin' Vacations

To maintain MACK DADDY status, it's crucial that while you reconfigure your life for your new heir, you retain those elements of your life that made you the hipster that you are. In other words, *don't* grow tits like Lactating Daddy or grow a bobble neck like Rubber-Stamp Daddy.

One of life's absolute necessities is the vacation. Many new parents get so bogged down and battered by an infant, they lose all sense of self. One day, they take the kid to kindergarten and on the way home, realize they haven't been out of town in six years.

When my daughter was about a year old, we decided we needed a few days away. Palm Springs was the destination. There was a hotel we'd always wanted to try—very Arabian Nights and heavily patronized by the Hollywood crowd. The moment the staff saw our tot, we got the stinkeye.

Now, some kids' behavior merits dirty looks. Parents who let their brats run wild, throw six-hour tantrums, and piss in the pool should be thrown out. But Olivia never made a sound and was barely walking. Yet, the service was surly . . . but not sufficiently overt to ignite a confrontation (subtle contempt is a Hollywood art form). A polite call for more towels took 25 minutes while we shivered by the pool. Our meals were served slow and cold while others around us were fawned over. The place just sucked. The morning we checked out, Olivia was naked, prancing around our room on tippy-toe. Suddenly, she squatted and took a hot, steaming dump in the middle of the Ali Baba sisal rug. Since there was no "tell us how you enjoyed your stay" card in the desk drawer, I was tempted to leave the turd to voice our opinion of the inn. Realizing some underpaid maid would be stuck with the chore, I cleaned up. But it seemed our daughter was on our wavelength.

So maybe a bed-and-breakfast with Hollywood A-listers wasn't the best place for a kid, but what do you do for R&R? Does having a kid consign you to Disneyland/Walt Disney World/Disney Cruises? If that's what blows up your skirt, then anchors away.

To me, kid vacations are nutty. Is your *kid* the one imprisoned in an office 50 weeks a year? Seems the parents are the ones needing the vacation. That's not to say you leave the kids home—if you did that, why did you have a family in the first place? It's about balance. Though I've never been, people tell me a Disney cruise is a lot like Chuck E. Cheese's at sea. Is that the relaxing experience you need to decompress from *Battlefield: Workplace?*

I can take only about four hours of the Happiest Place on Earth and that's at 4–6 year intervals. Once upon a time it wasn't that way. Old Uncle Walt knew that if he wanted the kiddies coming back, he'd better build in a few grins for the moms and dads. But, the new regime panders to political correctness and boundless greed. At every turn is another hustle for Mouse Merch. They even clip you a fistful of bucks for *parking*—like you're going to park in Disney's lot and then hike six miles to Knott's Berry Farm?

A theme-park visit is okay once in a while. Nothing wrong with climbing aboard some puke-inducing machine with your kid for a few screams and laughs. But to wrap an entire vacation around one?

A week at a Disney theme park could easily cost as much as a European vacation. When a Disney kid is in college and his pals who actually traveled overseas discuss their real world experiences, the Disney kid can chime in and recount his ride with the singing cardboard moppets of "It's a Small World."

Alternatives are everywhere. Every region of the country has something to offer, whether mountains, lakes, beaches, deserts, canyons, or cornfields. Those are the places that will feed your kid's imagination, curiosity, and soul, while taking far less jing from your wallet.

Day trips? How about a museum? Aquarium? Planetarium? A flea market, crafts fair, or concert in the park may have something worthwhile for you and your kids. You just never know.

All you need is the will to seek out your own fun, while telling the theme park suits to shove their canned kicks. Most local papers have a weekend or entertainment section that lists the coolest happenings around town. Check 'em out.

What are some MACK DADDY tricks to make journeying easier with the little ones? If it's the classic American car trip, load a cooler with fruit, sandwiches, and bottled water and whiz past those roadside emporiums of arterial plaque.

The toughest thing about road tripping with kids isn't getting fed, it's taking a leak. Highway rest areas are often abysmal. First, you have to pick your way through a minefield of dogshit as you walk through the parking lot. Next, beware of truckers using the area for a love nest. Then, once you get inside the bathroom, you need hip waders and a gas mask.

With kids, there's nothing restful about rest areas. Find a grassy area away from the parking lot, bring a ball for them to kick around, and let them burn off some energy for 15 or 20 minutes.

Air travel is another story. In the post-9/11 world, things can get ugly fast. Some airline people are pretty cool, and some are not. (On a recent trip, they made my 40-pound, sundress-wearing five-year-old remove her sandals because the buckles set off the metal detector.) What you want to do is get through security with as little hassle as possible, and with your laptop, camera, cell phone, and keys.

Here's the drill. Either you or your wife should wear *no metal whatsoever*. No belt or shoe buckles, put the Patek Philippe in her purse, wear drawstring pants, pocket change, etc. Also, wear slip-ons so you don't have to screw with laces.

Then, one of you walks through *first* and waits on the other side. Why? Because one of you needs to be there to watch your kids, not to mention all the valuable stuff you just put on the conveyor belt to be x-rayed. The security people aren't going to steal your stuff, but other nearsighted, harried, nervous, and just plain stupid travelers will pick up your stuff, thinking it's theirs, and walk off with it.

The idea is to get through to the plane without incurring any pat-downs, strip searches, or other Orwellian horseshit you may have to endure.

Once on the plane, here are a few things to think about. Infants ride on Mommy's lap, unless you buy a seat. If you buy a seat, you have to bring a car seat, because they won't allow you to buckle a baby into the airline seat. That's lot of extra bulk to lug. How interesting, that in a world we perceive as being kid-friendly, the airlines are telling us, "We don't give a rat's ass about your kid, unless of course, you want to pay for it." In the event of a crash, harsh landing, or extreme turbulence, your unsecured baby will fly through that cabin like a fleshy soccer ball. You can't buckle him on your lap—if you hit an air pocket, he'll be crushed. All you can do is try to hang on to him. Good luck.

Calamities aside, airplanes are probably filthier places than highway rest areas. It's a germ tube with a stagnant air supply and surfaces that see no disinfectant whatsoever. People sneeze, fart, cough, puke, lance carbuncles, and masturbate in those seats. And then we sit in them and eat. And small kids slobber on them.

Bring wipes and/or a plastic bottle of hand disinfectant. When you lower that tray table before feasting on that delicious selection of chicken or pasta, give the tray a wipe. Ditto your hands and most important, wipe the kids' hands several times throughout the flight.

Bring a bag full of busy shit, whether coloring books, puzzles, whatever the kid needs to keep him occupied. Cabin pressure can wreck your ears—one L.A.–N.Y. flight made me deaf in my left ear for several years. Think what that pressure feels like to your infant. When they commence the descent, try to have him sucking a bottle to lessen the pressure.

Bring some baby Tylenol. If your baby throws a fever at 35,000 feet, you're screwed without it. Bring a few diapers, and a complete change of clothes, in case he takes a soak-thru atomic dump.

Here's another air travel tip. Umbrella Stroller. They're light, fold small, and can really help you get around an airport with a baby. Some ball-breaking airline personnel enjoy forbidding them from entering the plane. (Oh what a *dangerous weapon!*) When they tell you that, say fine and let them keep the thing. You can buy a new one on the other end for 15 bucks.

About Dads, Well Said

"Sometimes the poorest man leaves his children the richest inheritance."—Ruth E. Renkel

"A father carries pictures where his money used to be."
—unknown

"It is a wise father that knows his own child."
—William Shakespeare

"It doesn't matter who my father was; it matters who I remember he was."—Anne Sexton

"Any man can be a father. It takes someone special to be a dad."—unknown

"When I was a boy of 14, my father was so ignorant I could hardly stand to have the old man around. But when I got to be 21, I was astonished at how much the old man had learned in seven years."—Mark Twain

"A wise son maketh a glad father . . ."—Proverbs 10:1

"I cannot think of any need in childhood as strong as the need for a father's protection."—Sigmund Freud

"The most important thing a father can do for his children is to love their mother."—David O. McKay

"Fatherhood is pretending the present you love most is soap-on-a-rope."—Bill Cosby

"There are three stages of a man's life: He believes in Santa Claus, he doesn't believe in Santa Claus, he is Santa Claus."—unknown

"What a father says to his children is not heard by the world, but it will be heard by posterity."—Jean Paul Richter

"Blessed indeed is the man who hears many gentle voices call him father!"—Lydia M. Child

"A truly rich man is one whose children run into his arms when his hands are empty."—unknown

"By the time a man realizes that maybe his father was right, he usually has a son who thinks he's wrong."
—Charles Wadworth

"It is a great moment in life when a father sees a son grow taller than he or reach farther."—Richard L. Evans

Battling Kid Consumerism

Newsweek magazine ran a cover story, HOW TO SAY "NO" TO YOUR KIDS . . . SETTING LIMITS IN AN AGE OF EXCESS.

How pathetic is this? A nice, deep economic recession will certainly ease the pain of saying no to a greedy brat. Barring that, how about a little old-fashioned denial?

Many parents claim the gimmes commence once the kid is in school and peer pressure kicks in. *But MO-OM, EVERYbody's got a cameraphone/iPOD/diaphragm/Lamborghini!*

Peer pressure is a part of it, but the behavior patterns that make kids susceptible are set when they're babies.

Long before kids get to school, their appetite for consumer crap has been whipped to a frenzy by television. Little ones stand on fat, wobbly legs staring at the latest hunk o' shit from Hazmatbro and say, "I want *dat!*" And many parents run right out and buy *dat.*

It's parents' responsibility to give kids a taste for quality—in food, entertainment, toys—everything. Let your child know that candy is crap. It will rot your teeth, stunt your growth, give you pimples, and make you stupid. At the same time, extol the virtues of apples, oranges, bananas, strawberries. For your daughter, it's "fruit is what Cinderella ate to make her beautiful." For a son, it's the Popeye and spinach/strength pitch. It worked for our daughter. She turns up her nose at Snickers but downs strawberries and grapes by the fistful.

At around age five, my daughter became very interested in Halloween. Other kids' front yards were strewn with store-bought ghosts, witches, Draculas, and so on. She wanted in on the fun, and why not? So I asked her which Halloween spook/monster/character she most dug. She really had no preference, so we opted for Frankenstein. Instead of heading into the Halloween super store, I suggested we build our own Frankenstein over the course of several weekends. She went nuts for the idea and pitched in with a resolve I'd never seen before. In other projects, her attention span was brief, but with this one, she became obsessed. From going through my old clothes to scouring the garage for scraps of wood to haunting thrift shops for the perfect Frankenstein boots (they were Kenneth Cole—barely worn—$8) it was all fun. Then there was building the frame, stuffing the clothes with plastic garbage bags (better than newspaper in case of rain).

As we progressed, her enthusiasm fueled my creativity. At first I thought I'd just slap together something fast and dirty—kind of a scarecrow with a Frankenstein mask on it. But pretty soon, as we both got into it, the monster grew to something worthy of Universal studios. After several weekends, "Uncle Frank" was christened at 6 feet 7 inches, with about a 56-inch chest. The eyes in his green face flashed with red lights. In his right hand, he clenched a glowing, bewigged skull, freshly decapitated. In his left, a two-foot butcher knife. How to properly display such a creation? We lashed him to the chimney with invisible monofilament.

It's amazing what a kid (and a dad) can learn while doing such a project. We built "Frank" flat on the ground. Standing him up, his legs were a little wobbly, but what the hell, he wasn't going dancing. However, the weight of the plastic garbage bags and clothing proved too much, and after hoisting Frank to the roof and lashing him to the chimney, he snapped at the hip and jackknifed forward.

Daddy learned to field-test such creations, while daughter learned a lesson about trial and error. So we rebuilt him—better. That night, we lit him up. He looked pretty intimidating.

Not long after Frank's completion, Olivia was asked to bring a recent family snapshot to nursery school. She insisted that I shoot one with Mommy, Daddy and "Uncle Frank." She wanted to be able to point to it and tell every other kid that she had built Uncle Frank with her dad. The total cash layout for this adventure was

about $30. But we both have a priceless memory. And, the neighbors seem to have a newfound respect (apprehension?) for me. While others found Uncle Frank a bit frightening—even gruesome, my daughter was completely unafraid. Is any mommy ever afraid of her own progeny?

The Frank scenario is one that can be applied across many spectrums. Of course, you probably can't build your kid his own iPod—but whenever possible, why not let him make his own fun?

Finally, Halloween arrived, and it was costume time. She wanted to be "Draclea" as she said. I could have had something whipped up by a studio costumer pal. Instead, it was off to the 99¢ store. One black vinyl cape with stand-up collar—99¢. One vampire makeup kit—99¢. She wore the cape around for a week before Halloween. Finally on the big night, we ripped open the bubble wrap on the makeup kit. It was crap—like trying to spread Play-Doh. (Whaddya want for 99¢?) Olivia said, "It doesn't matter, Daddy can fix it, he fixes *anything*!" There's one of the best MACK DADDY perks—automatic and unconditional confidence in your abilities as a super-hero regardless of how unfounded they may be.

As fate would have it, the fix-it was handed down from my own MACK DADDY. When I was trick-or-treating, my costume was always the same—a hobo. My old man would burn a cork, let it cool, and in two minutes he gave my seven-year-old face a deep five o'clock shadow. The burnt cork gave Olivia a nice widow's peak and Alice Cooper eyes.

There's always a reason to team up with your kids and create something for the moment and memories for a lifetime.

Watchism and the 3.75-Year Gift

Are you raising your kid as a Christian, Jew, Muslim, Buddhist, Shinto, whatever? Maybe not. Many children are being raised in the official religion of the United States—Watchism.

Watchism has eclipsed all other religions on the planet in only half a century. And why not? Who wants to attend the same old Mass every Sunday for an entire hour, or the same old service at the synagogue or mosque, when Watchism brings you any sport, movie, pay-per-view, fuck-flick, *OC* episode, Ron Popeil product demo, or glinting zircon ring hypnotically revolving on a blue velvet spindle? No contest, baby. Watchism rules.

Theologians and philosophers cry out in despair, "Where is our moral compass?" Answer: It was zapped into slag by the particle beams of the cathode ray tube.

Will Watchism make a kid a violent killer, a prostitute, or a drug addict? Probably not. But what it will do is inculcate him with not-so-subtle messages that may conflict with your beliefs.

You really have to monitor what your kids see on television—when you're in the house or your nanny/sitter/governess/grandma is.

For very young ones (under three), choose shows that are quiet and slow paced. *Blues Clues* and *Dora the Explorer* type shows are best. Little minds aren't ready to process the frenetic pacing and decibel levels of other cartoons. You don't need them torqued up by visual and audio overstimulation—you want them calm and engaged. If they learn something, that's a bonus. *Sesame Street* is okay, too.

Can you trust a channel? Many parents see mouse ears and think it's all good. Is it? While you won't see sex or gore on Disney, if you view the movies with an analytical eye, you *will* see not-so-subtle agendas being advanced. For instance, in *The Little Mermaid* and *Aladdin*, both Ariel and Jasmine dis Dad to date the stud of their choice. Of course, few fathers ever approve of their daughter's boyfriends, but the message to little girls is *Go chase that genie-panted/swashbuckling stud with the six-pack abs. If Dad has a problem with it, he can fuck off!* All good stories revolve around conflict, but why must that conflict be resolved by shitting on Dad? Yeah, yeah, same theme in *Romeo and Juliet*, but Shakespeare wasn't scribing his stuff for the under-12 market.

Plenty of Disney non-animated fare features preteen nymphettes in hot pants and bare midriffs singing about *love*.

Some of TV's offerings are outright banned in our house. No one in our home speaks dude, but I noticed my kid suddenly talking with the patois of a moron surfer. Answer: *Rocket Power*. This cartoon, that depicts a bunch of latchkey kids haunting the Santa Monica pier, is truly odious. Avoid it. Ditto *Rugrats*.

On the other hand, *SpongeBob SquarePants* manages—as so few do—to entertain both generations. It is usually brilliant—funny, smart, pure entertainment with no hidden agenda. My daughter and I howl at the show.

Thanks to Watchism, we have a generation of American kids who are overweight, indolent, and unaccomplished. They can't play an instrument, but they can dress, perforate, and tattoo themselves just like the latest MTV "it boy". They can't shoot hoops but they know the graphic sexual peccadilloes of their NBA role models. They can't throw a spiral or run a button hook, but they know exactly how their favorite defensive lineman stacks his steroids.

Are our athletes and entertainers to blame? Hell no. They are merely well-paid deacons in the cult of Watchism. The blame is on us.

When Mark McGwire set a new home run record, and was then accused of using steroids, some idiot fan accosted him. "How could you DO this? You are my son's role model!" To which McGwire replied, "Why the hell aren't YOU your son's role model?" Damn straight, Mark. Neither Mark, nor any other professional athlete, musician, or actor is obliged to hold themselves to any "higher standard." If McGwire chose to take the field with Decabol-filled syringes bobbing from his eyeballs, that was between Mark and his employers.

A MACK DADDY is his son's role model. If together they enjoy watching great athletes play, that's terrific. But beware letting him get caught up in hero worship, because as we've seen again and again, you just never know when that hero's going to morph into a punk. Let your kid know that's just a man on the field—a fast/agile/strong/talented man, but a man nonetheless.

Between your kid's birth and eighteenth year, you have the demigod power to endow him with nearly four extra years. Is this a parlor trick? No. The average family watches five hours per day, that's 76 days per year. Over 18 years that will accrue to 3.75 YEARS—*years!!* And 3.75 years is enough time to do damn near anything—go to law or medical school, become a movie star, rock star, get a company off the ground. And that's for adults. For kids, imagine what can be accomplished with that extra 35 hours . . . per week.

We have become a nation of passive, pathetic watchers. And what we're watching is mostly shit. It matters not whether it's nighttime teen soaps or the evening news. Everyone plays it fast and loose with the facts. News has all the veracity of the WWF—because "info-tainment" is just fine.

No one would think it odd to walk into someone's home and see a mezuzah on the doorpost or a crucifix on the wall or a religious shrine in a corner. But if there were religious iconography in every room *and* the family vehicles, you might think them strange, no?

Q. *Where is the god of Watchism?*

A. *TV/god is everywhere. In the living room, dining room, and every bedroom, in the playoom, kitchen and in the headrests of the Lexus.*

Families that practice Watchism do so with a zeal uncommon for any religion—in this or any century or hemisphere. Their five-hour daily minimum increases on high-viewing days of obligation—Olympics, Playoffs, Super Bowls, World Series, Awards Ceremonies, Sitcom special events, (lesbian kisses, weddings, births, farewell episodes).

There's nothing wrong with *some* television. It's not all bad—once in a while it can be outstanding. Five hours a week might be a better viewing schedule than five hours a day.

Spanking

There's an incendiary word. No doubt knife fights have broken out when adults argue about spanking. It's a thorny subject that needs some examination. Many years ago, it was considered standard practice—for everyone from toddlers to fraternity pledges. Now, it's a highly charged, yet unsettled subject.

Should you spank your child? If so, when and how?

Spanking as a general form of discipline doesn't work. It is, after all, violence and there's usually a smarter way to handle behavior problems.

There are, however, circumstances when a smack on a toddler's butt may be the *only* way to modify his behavior. A two-year-old kid who wriggles free from your hand and darts into the street doesn't understand that an automobile will maim or kill him. This may be a time when a whack on the behind makes a point he may otherwise not understand.

I recall the first and only time I ever spanked my older daughter. She, her mommy, and I were shopping in a department store. Olivia was about three years of age. One second she was standing between us, the next she was gone—as if vaporized. Frantically, we searched the immediate area, shouting her name. Slowly, we broadened our search, and realized we were close to the exit which led into a vast mall. Had she ventured out into it?

Strangers began to call out to us, saying, "There's a kid over here," and, "I think I saw a kid around here a minute ago."

Never, ever in my life, did I feel such fear. Had some murderous pedophile snatched my baby? Though her disappearance probably lasted no more than two minutes, it was an eternity. A final stake of terror was driven through my heart when some clerk, in an effort to console us said—"Don't worry, we'll check the videotapes after closing." At that moment, I truly thought I would die. Then we heard Olivia giggle. She stood not ten feet from us. She had been hiding in a rack of clothing the whole time. I began to breathe again. I got on my knees, grabbed her and said, "Don't you ever *ever* hide from Mommy and me, and if we call you, you *answer!*" I made my point by swatting her butt. She burst into tears. From then on, Olivia shadowed us whenever we left the house. And I had no regrets whatsoever about the single spank I gave her. What would have been the alternative? A dialog? *Olivia, there are sick, less-than-human people called pedophiles. They take little children like you and use, torture and dismember them and throw their body parts into dumpsters. So, please, keep us apprised of your whereabouts at all times.*

If your toddler is determined to chin himself on the hot barbecue, or put his fist through a bee hive, or anything else that could put him in a burn unit or morgue—yeah—spank him once to make the point. But if he leaves his trike in the driveway or writes on the walls or throws your wallet in the toilet—dialog and some nonviolent punishment is the way to go.

If you make a threat, make good on it. Otherwise nothing you say will be taken seriously.

Remember, young minds can only process so much information. I laugh when I overhear parents talking to their 18-month-olds at the supermarket. *No, Madison, we're not buying Sugar Grenades—they're too high in fructose and hydrogenated emulsifiers. Let's look at these nice legumes over here in produce.*

Before you take a kid to task for bad behavior always consider first the two reasons to let bad behavior slide—fatigue and hunger. If they are either, they need sleep or food—not punishment.

Coach Fuehrer

Sometimes they're called "helicopter parents" because of the way they hover over their kids. They come in both sexes, but we're talking dads here, so . . .

As a kid, I played the usual urban sports in NYC. There was no nearby "sandlot" and Little League was pretty much unheard of. So we'd choose a street with relatively less traffic. Nobody owned any base bags, so we'd designate objects to represent bases. Home plate and second base were manhole covers. First base was the left rear fender of a Buick. Third base was the left front fender of a Pontiac.

The bat was a stickball bat. You could buy one in the store, but we preferred to make our own—a sawed-off broom handle, one end wrapped with gaffer's or duct tape. A kid with a good swing could make the damn thing whistle as he swatted. If he'd hit the ball solidly near the tip, it would go into orbit.

The ball was either a Pennsy Pinkie or a Spalding (always pronounced, in New York parlance, *Spawl-deen*). There were endless arguments over which brand would bounce higher and hit farther. The Pennsy was the color of salmon and very smooth. Over time, it would definitely hold its bounce longer. They'd lose their firmness, but it seemed they'd never completely "go dead." (Legend has it that a Pennsy Pinkie did go into orbit when John Glenn took one aboard his Mercury capsule for exercise and stress relief.)

Spaldings, on the other hand, seemed to dry out and "go dead" more quickly. However, in their youth, they had a decided advantage over the Pennsy Pinkies. The Spaldings actually had a bit of a grain to their rubber surface, facilitating a better grip and, in a skilled hand, the ability to throw them on a curve.

Usually, we lacked sufficient kids to field a catcher (and who would be crazy enough to get behind a guy swinging four to five feet of broom handle, anyway?), so we played "fungo"—you pitched to yourself.

We had the greatest times you could possibly imagine. In summer, some of those games would go from early Saturday morning until the ball was obscured in darkness. They were fabulous. Nobody was ever hit by a car—there was never even a close call, because there were sharp eyes in every direction, but most important—we all liked the hell out of each other. The "team" aspect of play was almost meaningless, because it seemed the teams would shift by the game. There were very few fights— we were just kids having a great time with other kids. We never, even for a second, sought the help, advice, or intervention of any adult. What the hell for? Play was for play. We got all the adult supervision we could stand at school and home. When we were out on the street, it was kids only—total freedom—and adults were *not* welcome.

When somebody'd really put the wood to the ball, it would slice through the highest boughs of the Dutch elms and maples that lined the street, and would actually sever some leaves or branches. We'd hear the sound of the cracking wood, look up, and go, "Holy shit, Lenny, what a hit," as we watched the leaves fall to earth. Many times, balls would vanish and we'd suspend play for however long it took to retrieve them. We'd hop fences, climb roofs, out-run watchdogs, poke around in backyards—the adventure of locating the ball could be more fun than the game. I recall seeing a ball disappear beneath a Chevy and sliding under for a look. I finally found it—wedged in by the ball joints.

When we'd get thirsty, we'd find an unguarded garden hose and glug from it.

Today, I drive past perfectly manicured ball fields in Los Angeles and see kids in full MLB regalia, shin guards and helmets and cleats and snappy uniforms and batting gloves and orange coolers full of Gatorade and an adjacent parking lot full of Navigators and Escalades packed with pro-grade baseball paraphernalia and every three feet, another adult, hovering, shouting advice or arguing with coaches and I think to myself . . . *is that fun?*

When do kids get a chance to just be kids? To wolf down dinner, explode out the front door, and hook up with your pals for some pure adventure.

About the only time I become envious of kids is when I see the skateboarders. Occasionally, I'll spot a pack of them loping through the streets like stray dogs, in their T-shirts and baggy pants and no helmets or equipment and I'll think, *Where are the meddling adults to ruin their fun?* Answer: street-boarding is pretty much an un-organized pastime without rules, coaches, or protocols. And, most adults will break their asses if they try to keep up with their kids.

Adults bring an intensity to games that children don't. I recall playing golf (under duress, mind you) with the publisher of a very prestigious magazine and two of his lieutenants at a toney New England course. Somewhere around the 12th hole, an electrical storm came up from nowhere. I headed for the club-house in a downpour, while they played on, soaked to their BVDs as fork lightning flashed like mortar fire. Later that day, they actually gave me static about walking off the course.

My brother had a similar experience while watching his nine-year-old play soccer in a thunderstorm, and got a ration of shit from the coach when he pulled his son off the field. (This earned the foolish coach a much larger ration of shit from my brother.) And how about the Texan who recently shot his son's football coach? It's insane.

Sport isn't the only arena where dads ramrod their kids to proficiency. A current big trend in NYC is for Wall Street fat cats who only hire nannies bilingual in Mandarin. Why? Because mainland China is *the* burgeoning economic power, and speaking their language will give Junior an edge when he's starting out at Goldman Sachs.

America is a land obsessed with self-improvement. For decades, novels topped best-seller lists—juicy, satisfying escapist fiction. Novels have been replaced by self-help. How to make yourself thinner, richer, stronger, sexier, more attractive, more spiritual, efficient, successful, how to get laid (guys), how to get married (women).

This obsession with self-improvement and perfection doesn't just trickle down to children; it lands on them with a crushing thud.

Remember when summer camp was a place where city and suburban kids went to paddle a canoe, swim, climb trees, ride a horse, catch fireflies, toast marshmallows, and tell ghost stories by the campfire?

Check out summer camps now. It's easy to believe there's a camp for every conceivable sport. But would you believe Computer Camp, Acting Camp, Science Camp, Stuntman Camp, Rock Star Camp, Cheerleading and Dance Camp, Filmmaking, Claymation & Digital Animation Camp (bet that's an L.A. anomaly), or how about, yes folks, I shit you not, *Money Camp!*

A MACK DADDY mantra is to help a kid find his bliss. But clearly, loads of Der Fuehrer Daddies are resurrecting abandoned or stunted dreams and force-feeding them to their kids. How many eight-year-old kids say, "Dad, I wanna learn about fixed debentures. Will you send me away to Money Camp, please?"

Of course, if your eight-year-old went trick-or-treating in a green eyeshade and sleeve garters, then obviously, Money Camp is where he should be.

Stage mothers (and dads) abound in show business. The whole JonBenet Ramsey circuit is alive and well. Here's a survey for the pollsters. Find out what percentage of kids who play games/sports supervised and organized by adults don't actually wish they were someplace else.

Not too long ago at my gym, I watched a Der Fuehrer Dad "train" his kid, who appeared to be about 12 years of age. The guy was really in his face and barking at him, like some Parris Island D.I.

There are varying schools of thought about weight lifting and kids. Some experts claim it will inhibit growth and is better left until the kid is full grown. Others say it's all good and you're never too young to start.

I recall my own tastes at that age. *Go to a stinking, sweaty gym with a bunch of grunting geezers instead of being outside in the sun with my friends, playing tag or stick ball? Are you nuts?* I never entered a gym until I was in my 20s and imprisoned in an office all day. By the time I got home from work on a winter's night, all the other kids on the block were finished playing tag.

But this guy was really putting his son through his paces, and the boy clearly was not enjoying himself. Der Fuehrer Dad had all the right gear—fancy weight belt, fingerless gloves, braces at every joint, and a sleeveless muscle shirt. Equipment notwithstanding, he was still a spaghetti-armed, pencil-necked guy. He couldn't grow any significant muscle, but *godammit, his son would!*

(There are now grassroots programs that address how fed-up people are with hyper-competitive parents. In parts of Southern California they've instituted Silent Soccer, whereby parents and coaches are effectively muzzled, allowing kids to play without their intrusive exhortations. They call them soccer mums.)

Nobody wants their kid to be a latch-key kid. You want to be involved and know what he or she is up to. Despite the endless assault of government-sponsored commercials to the contrary, every kid with an unsupervised hour on his hands isn't out looking for a warm spike full of China White. Part of being a kid is goofing off, exploring on your own, and enjoying being a small person on this spinning globe.

Unless your kid is an enormously talented artist or inventor or prophetic investor, he or she will spend a lifetime *competing*. Is it necessary to cultivate a killer instinct while he's still sucking his thumb?

When my first daughter was born, someone called to "congratulate" me. Within the same breath, she asked me what her APGAR scores were.

I had no idea what she was talking about. All I knew was that my baby was beautiful and healthy.

"What's an APGAR score," I asked.

She snorted at my ignorance.

This woman was always trying to keep a competitive tally by asking outrageously nosey questions about my income, investments, home value, prices paid for automobiles, and so on. She had recently become a mom and the subtext of her APGAR question was, *I want to know if my kid is better than your kid*. Wow.

Hey Kids, Let's Party!

Maybe my parents were kind of austere, maybe they were frugal, or maybe they just had their heads screwed on straight. I wasn't raised by Cotton Mather, but hasn't the kiddie party thing gotten way out of hand?

When I was four or five my brother and I (three years my senior but just a few week's birth date from mine) had one party covering both birthdays. I doubt that Mom got two cakes—she probably had me blow out five candles, then re-lit and added three for my brother. There were party hats, there were rolling noisemakers, there was tri-color ice cream and it was all over in an hour or two. There were maybe ten kids there, total—just my bro's and my crew. We wolfed down some cake and then, in a fructose frenzy, headed outside to jump around like fleas in a jar.

The last thing we wanted was our parents (or any *adult*) coordinating our fun.

Imagine my surprise when I attended a fourth birthday party for one of my daughter's nursery school friends. This kid is not the child of some corporate mogul—her dad is a middle manager and Mom stays at home. I counted almost a hundred people in attendance. (How many people does *your* four-year-old know?) The theme (*themes* are de rigueur) was Bob the Builder. So . . . there were Bob the Builder cups, napkins, and paper plates, a Bob the Builder Cake (sized to serve a construction crew for the Hoover Dam), an actual Bob the Builder character dressed in coveralls and yellow hardhat with his femme assistant (she stressed the denim on her coveralls quite nicely) giving lessons on how to check if a door jam is plumb, and a Bob the Builder inflatable bouncy house. There was also a guy (sans construction garb) with a pony giving rides to any kid that wanted one. Of course, being in reasonable proximity to Hollywood, there were take-away gift bags, which I half expected to contain BlackBerries and Cartier watches.

What did this cost, I wondered? I looked at the birthday boy. He seemed as thrilled by his Bob the Builder theme party as a porn star at a quilting bee. I wanted to take him by the hand and walk him around the yard and ask him the name of every kid in attendance. Odds are, he would have known fewer than 10 percent. Because not only did Mommy invite every kid in his nursery school class, but every kid in the nursery *school*, so as not to be "exclusionary." Oh good. The political correctness begins even at nursery school.

So what are these parties about? Are they about parents flaunting affluence? Displaying their devotion to the kid? Vicarious wish fulfillment? After the massive cleanup and equally massive bills, how much would the birthday boy recall about his fourth birthday?

Of course, birthdays are limited and celebrating them is the right thing to do. But with an infant or tot, sensory overload always looms large.

Try something smaller and more manageable. Around my daughter's fifth, she became obsessed with Alice in Wonderland. She'd recently attended a number of birthday extravaganzas and of course wanted one of her own. So my wife devised one and the theme was Alice. The whole thing came off for about a hundred bucks.

I hung oversized picture playing cards (Target—$4) from the ceiling (monofilament, the MACK DADDY's best friend). Instead of flying in the pastry chef from Cote Basque, my wife and daughter baked their own cupcakes and let each kid decorate them themselves. Three foot-long subs from the supermarket deli filled the adult bellies ($30). There were balloons, face painting, and musical chairs.

What there was not, was chaos, injury, or fights. Of course, if some fifth graders found out about the party, they may have felt "excluded." Tsk, tsk.

(A good rule of thumb may be not to invite any more kids than your kid's age—if he's turning five, invite five kids—that's about all he can handle.)

My daughter thoroughly enjoyed herself, despite the lack of a bouncy house, a pony, adult costumed characters, and scores of kids she didn't know. And she even learned something. Kids form strange attachments. For some reason, my daughter was enamored with another little girl from her school. Neither my wife nor I could fathom the attraction, which was entirely one-sided. Little Danielle was sullen, unresponsive, and downright weird. At the party, Danielle refused to participate in anything— she just sat and sulked. After several attempts to cajole her into the spirit, Olivia abandoned the kid and played happily with the other kids.

Within a few weeks, I noticed talk of her "best friend" Danielle had ceased. When I asked about it, Olivia told me she was through with her. "Why," I asked.

"Daddy, don't you think she was rude at my party?" That made the party worth the hundred bucks—cubed.

New Best Friends . . . Every Week

Kids are worse than the most annoying cruise ship social director. They latch on to "friends" at school, and suddenly you're hanging out at BBQs with total strangers. Several times, I found myself socializing with other parents and got this feeling of déjà vu. I'd seen these people before . . . on *COPS*.

How did today's parents (we) get roped into interface with the parents of their playmates? When I was a kid back in New York, my old man never, ever met the parents of the kids I ran with. Why the hell would he? You met kids around the neighborhood, which were pretty much the same kids you met at school. You played stickball, touch football, and *I Declare War* with them. Then Mom called you from the window or stoop. You went inside for dinner and that was it until the next day. Nobody owned a watch or a calendar or a text-messaging cell phone. . . . We just sort of naturally *coalesced* the way those last few Cheerios always seem to clump in the bowl. When and more importantly, how did this *play date* horseshit begin?

In Los Angeles, where everything and everyone is fake, people's front yards are in fact *façades* . . . something just for show. Despite the fab weather, domestic lives are lived indoors or in the backyard. Maybe that's the problem here—since no one ever, ever hangs out in *front* of their home, everybody might as well be in another zip code. They glide in and out of their garages in window-tinted rides like OPEC oil ministers. Kids only meet one another through properly arranged introductions. It's Victorian. And it's unnatural.

The mothers get along much better than the dads do. They've been practicing forced gaiety and bogus affection since *they* were little girls. They "play nice" with the other mommies. The guys, on the other hand, couldn't give a rat's ass. Like you really want to get to know Tiffany Koplotnick's old man, and get his pitch on term versus whole? Usually, there's a wide-screen TV somewhere on the premises, and the dads cluster around it, feigning interest in some lame game.

One MACK DADDY play is to make a toothy cameo, then retreat to your automobile with a magazine, book, or the cell phone. What's the point in getting to know these guys? By Monday, your kid hates his kid's guts and has anointed a new "best friend."

Women, being the meddlesome social engineers that they are, want nothing more than to have *everyone* "play nice." If they wrote the rules to baseball, anyone who stepped up to the plate would advance to second base just for having his shirt tucked in. Everyone would win, too. (Except when it came to who had the biggest tits, best hair, nicest shoes/tennis bracelet/husband/boyfriend with the biggest wallet/job/cock . . . *then* they get *competitive*.)

So, Olivia is in nursery school and has assembled a posse of little friends. A few of the mommies get together over double-decaf vanilla lattes and decide spousal male bonding is compulsory. I find myself driving 15 miles to play cards with a half-dozen guys I don't know.

I arrive at this home and the acrimony between host and hostess is so highly charged, it may generate ball lightning. (There was subsequently a divorce.) Through clenched teeth, they argue about the platter of appetizers. Then the wife splits for girls' night out with the rest of the hens, leaving us boys to "play nice."

Somebody produces a deck of cards and some chips, and now it's time to ante up. The conversation is stilted, boring shit like you might find at a multi-divisional offsite.

"How's your third-quarter shaping up, Mike?"

"It was a little soft, but since we signed on the new distributor, we're on fire."

"Our IT guy says we need new servers, but I dunno . . ."

I am in *pain*.

I have friends who are fascinated by serial killers. Years ago, we challenged one another to shoehorn into every conversation, business or personal, no matter how irrelevant, the name *Charles Manson*. I flash on that memory and wonder if I should answer the challenge now. Screw it, these dweebs'll never get it. So I pretty much shut up and play.

One yo-yo shows up an hour late and empty handed. (Poker etiquette says at least bring a six-pack for the gang.) He grabs a beer and stuffs his face from the platter. When they tell him to ante up, he says he has no money.

I *must* ask, and do, "Did you know this was a card game?"

"Yes, but I didn't think it was for *money*," he replies, with bound-less contempt.

This was *not* my crowd.

I split.

Once home, as I always do, I headed for Olivia's room first. I tell my wife it's to be sure she hasn't kicked the covers off (which she invariably does) but she knows the truth—I love looking at her and when I'm away from her for any length of time, I just need to breathe the same air. As I watched her breathe those deep breaths of deep sleep, I smiled. Someday, *she* would groove on the Charles Manson challenge.

Not only must you be ready to deal with the forced parental socialization, sometimes the kids themselves are positively hemorrhoidal. Kids become infatuated with other kids—and sometimes that other kid *is* Charles Manson. This is a conundrum.

I recall when I was about five briefly palling with a kid of about eight or nine. This kid constantly played with matches and that included setting fire to things, like fence posts or somebody's front door.

One afternoon, my Irish immigrant, tough-as-nails grandfather was babysitting me and got an eyeful of me and my junior-arsonist pal. We were in the backyard; I was watching him trying to ignite something—I think it was the garage. Suddenly the backdoor flew open so hard, it smacked the wall behind it.

"You, firebug! Get your ass outta here now!" Grandpa roared.

The Human Torch left a comet tail as he fled.

"Larry, inside." Grandpa's massive thumb jerked over his shoulder.

In the house, he gave me a good talking-to about choosing my friends. Obviously, he put it in terms my five-year-old brain could process—it sank in. He laid it out for me in plain English—"That kid is sick in the head. . . . The fire he starts could kill people—maybe even you. . . . Keep away from him—forever!"

What would today's child behaviorists say about the way Grandpa handled the situation? They'd say he should have politely asked the other boy's name and phone number, then called his parents and explained the situation. Perhaps they could meet over a frappuccino and *explore* a list of therapists who specialize in helping children that *act out* in this way. Was it a syndrome or a disorder that troubled the child? Maybe they could have an intervention (or at least a time-out) and commence the healing process.

Grandpa handled the situation perfectly. Arson is a crime and an arsonist is a criminal. And back then, seven was considered the age of reason, when any kid playing with a full deck should be able to discern right from wrong. Sending that little punk packing, with a bolt of fear lodged in his warped head—was the right thing to do.

Many years later, I still berate myself for not acting in the style of my wise, ballsy Grandpa. My daughter (at age 2½) had become friends with a nice little girl of her own age. This little girl had an older sister of about 6 or 7, named Constance. She was spoiled and obnoxious. Regardless of how outrageous her behavior, her air-headed mommy and daddy would smile and say, "She's so precocious." One day, we went to the park with them and the kids. There was a decorative fountain nearby, stagnant with islands of congealed algae and pigeon shit.

This was not our first outing with these people. I'd seen Constance pull some nasty stunts and then lie about them. I neither liked nor trusted this kid. But we didn't want to deprive Olivia of the company of the younger sister, who was a sweet little thing.

Olivia and Constance were at the fountain. I looked over to see Constance scooping filthy water from it with a Frisbee and offering it to Olivia to drink. I bolted and snatched the Frisbee, telling Constance, "Don't give this to Olivia to drink—it could make her very sick." The bitch rolled her eyes and smirked at me with *fuck you, asshole* contempt, then pranced away.

I looked at Olivia, trying to figure if she'd ingested any of the water. She said she hadn't, but she was only 2½. I couldn't be sure.

Ten minutes later, the same scene replayed. I was apoplectic. As before, Constance wasn't drinking any *herself*—she knew exactly what she was doing.

This time I was too late. Olivia had gulped a mouthful.

I wanted to grab Constance and dunk her ugly head (yeah, PC people, kids can be ugly—where do you think ugly adults come from?) in that fountain until she had sucked down a few quarts, à la Jim Carrey in *Me, Myself & Irene*.

I wanted to seize her space-shot daddy by his permed, peroxide-tipped hair and tell him, "Hey, Moonbeam, your kid isn't precocious, she's an obnoxious little bitch, and you better get her under control!"

On the drive home, Olivia was burning up with fever. What type of disease had she contracted from that fountain? What parasites, amoebas, or Christ knew what else was festering in it? I silently cursed Constance and her stupid, permissive parents, but mostly I cursed myself, first for not keeping a closer eye on Olivia. Then, more rationally, for not having forbidden any play whatsoever with Constance.

What's the MACK DADDY point? Never, ever hesitate to insult, alienate, or verbally assault anyone . . . in service to your child's welfare. Thankfully, Olivia quickly recovered from the tainted water. Just a few years later, I can barely recall the names or faces of *precocious* Constance's parents, whom in those days, we considered not friends but acceptable acquaintances.

The MACK DADDY moral is: Friends come and go. Worry not about them *nor* their feelings *nor* their kids' feelings.

Your *kids* are forever and come first—always.

When Your Little Machiavelli Tries to Divide and Conquer

Kids are far more perceptive than we realize. When tensions flare with Mommy and you both think you're keeping a lid on it with modulated voices and coded arguments . . . they *know*. They may not grasp the context, but when discord triumphs over harmony . . . they know.

Kids are also surprisingly adept politicians. What do they want? What they want. How will they get it? Any way they can. They will intuitively try to pit one parent against the other. If you allow this to happen, you are doomed.

By the time a kid is 2½ or 3 years old, he'll say, "Daddy, can I have some ice cream?" If you say "no," then he'll look to Mom. "Mommy, can I have some ice cream?"

MACK DADDIES and mommies must always, always present a united front. If your child says Daddy, can I have an ice cream, ask him if he's already asked Mommy. If he has and she's said no, say no, too. Even if he's screaming, don't give in. Once you do, everyone loses.

This is especially difficult if you're both simmering over some unsettled argument . . . that's when you may slip and contradict the other's wishes, just for the hell of it. Bad move. The victory will be fleeting and the real loser will be the kid.

A kid's emotional antenna is most sensitive to changes in environmental stability. Stability and consistency are what they crave and need to flourish. The domestic "controlled chaos" advocates are dead wrong. Do you enjoy the "controlled chaos" (translation: uncertainty) resulting when your company has been acquired by another and you spend nights wondering if you'll be shit-canned this Friday? Or, how would you dig the uncertainty of waiting for a biopsy? Not very appealing. And you're a MACK DADDY, a man of the world, a guy with some miles on his odometer. How does uncertainty feel to a three-, four-, or five-year-old? Probably something like raw terror.

People with marriages that work invariably share more similar-ities than differences. Opposites may attract, but only until the novelty wears off. If you and the old lady are at odds on everything from ketchup versus mustard to who should be in the White House, get some help on getting your act together for the baby. When it comes to your kid, you need to be in lockstep. Nothing will screw up a child quicker than parental discord.

When the wheels come off a marriage, that's when people need to be most vigilant, but all too often, the child becomes a pawn in a battle of the gimmes.

Marriage without kids is nothing but dating with a contract. If you decide to pull the plug, so what? But once there's a child involved, it gets all too real. When I was single and made it my business to talk with as many young, attractive women as possible, one thing was obvious right off the bat, and that was if they were from a broken home. Invariably they had an uneasy, guarded way about them. Don't let that be part of your legacy to your child.

Before people marry, discussions about children are usually as brief as *Do you want kids/how many?* Before your baby is out of diapers, you and your wife should have a talk about how you plan to raise that kid—just to see if your views are parallel or divergent. Throw around some tough questions you may have to tackle down the line. Stuff like, *Junior's being bullied at school, how should we handle it?* Or, *Junior aced the fifth grade math final, and we know he can't add six and five.* Or, *fourteen-year-old Madison wants to become sexually active, what to do?*

Thanksgiving

Since I don't have much family in California, I've attended many Thanksgiving dinners at the homes of friends. Sometimes, I've been astounded at the way I've seen this uniquely American holiday distorted. The first Thanksgiving, of course, was for Pilgrims to celebrate survival. One can envision a few hardy Puritans gathered around a long table in a candlelit, drafty log house, sharing the bounty of a harvest.

Over time, Thanksgiving became a reason for geographically fragmented families to gather. The meal was merely an excuse for people to get close to each other and fill in the blanks of their lives created by time and distance.

Now, it's become a chance for people to share space and food, but not each other.

Let me illustrate my point with a thumbnail of a genuine late-November holiday.

My fondest Thanksgiving memory is one at my Uncle John's in upstate New York's Catskill Mountains. One of his sons drove his family in from Albany. The other from Chicago. My mom, dad, brother, and I made the 120-mile trip from NYC. There was a long table laid in the middle of his living room. For three days, everyone hunkered down and feasted, laughed, drank, sang, and told stories. There were thrilling late-night runs over icy roads to pizzerias. The incendiary, greasy boxes were thrown into the fireplace and we wondered if we'd burn the house down. There were good-natured political arguments, fishing and hunting tales, and loads of advice from the adults to the kids. Uncle John put a Burl Ives LP on his cherry-wood console stereo Hi-Fi system and rushed the season a little with a few Christmas carols. My cousin's pregnant wife held my six-year-old hand to her belly so I could feel my second cousin kick.

Come Sunday morning, as car trunks were slammed between hugs and handshakes, eyes were moist and throats were lumpy.

If there was a television turned on during that long, wonderful weekend, I don't remember it.

Though separated by thousands of miles, we stayed in touch and still have great affection for one another. Uncle John has been gone a long time, but his sons, their families, and mine remain close.

Now the custom seems to be, strafe a buffet, then hit the couch with a plate balanced on your knees and watch . . . *the game*. It's mind-blowing. People will drive hundreds of miles (or fly thousands) investing time and money to be with their relatives, so they can watch . . . *the game*. Which is actually several games on Thanksgiving—isn't it?

Are we so terrified of conversation and the occasional silence it may bring that the TV *must* provide 24/7 white noise/background-fill?

When your kid's a teenager and asks what Grandpa was like, you may not have a clue, but you *will* be able to describe, in minute detail, an end-run by some tailback from Georgia Tech.

At Thanksgiving in my home, I've had guests throw flimsy excuses and leave in a huff when they were informed we didn't plan on watching any games that day.

But it's not really about sports or television or the Internet. Kids grow up. Older family members (sometimes younger) die. If you take the trouble to visit or host them, why not do it right? TiVo the game and watch it when you get home.

If you're doing the hosting, why not establish some MACK DADDY traditions of your own? Get Grandma or Grandpa to reminisce about their favorite holidays. Tape a prize under a random chair and let the winner sing a song or tell a story or do a trick to redeem it. Instead of standard dessert, build a bonfire or spark up the BBQ and roast marshmallows.

Here's a real wild idea—after dinner, instead of watching the game, grab the pigskin, go outside, and *have* a game. Everybody can participate—small kids can cheerlead, older folks can referee or keep score. If everyone's too bloated for football, make it horseshoes—tons o' fun and you'll never break a sweat. These are the things family memories are made of, and help give a kid a sense of belonging.

Happy Hellidays!

At best, they are unsatisfying. At worst, they can be minefields littered with broken dreams and shattered expectations. Who's to blame? Partly we are and partly Charles Dickens, Hallmark, and Currier & Ives. No other time of year holds such promise and can deliver such disappointment. For centuries, Christmas holidays were treacherous emotional waters to be navigated only by Christians. Now, thanks to boundless corporate greed layered with homogenizing multiculturalism and all-inclusive political correctness, people of *all* faiths are commanded to have a "Happy Holiday" or go bankrupt trying.

(The holiday insanity reaches a secondary flashpoint at New Year's Eve—another bungee pit for rocky relationships and battered egos. From your teens, you are expected to have *the greatest party night of your life*. And at 12 midnight, you better have a lip-lock on a super model or you're a worthless stain. Or, if you've been dating someone more than a month—*time to commit*!)

Who among us can recall a Christmas that met our expectations? Of course, the early childhood ones seem like they were best—we lacked the acuity to spot flaws, strife, and family dysfunction. Ignorance is bliss—especially at the Yuletide season.

When the "Season's Greetings" vortex of spend-and-give swirls your way this December, will you handle it differently now that you're a father?

If you had some good holiday memories as a kid, you can try to replicate them. But beware—the warm and fuzzy experience you seek may be conjured only within your imagination. Your 1- to 12-month-old baby will not grasp the concept of gifts. He may be dazzled by the lights and ornaments, but he's not going to recognize the scent of mulled spice or request another chorus of "White Christmas." And the mountain of toys arriving from Grandma and Grandpa will be in a Goodwill bin by mid-spring. Best plan of action is to do it up the way you want and then, getting baby tucked in as early as possible, enjoy the evenings and the season with your wife.

Years one–five will determine how your kids will perceive and deal with the holidays for the rest of their lives. If your memories of early holidays don't bring a smile to your face, now's your chance to do it your way and maybe establish some family traditions that will give your kid the warm and fuzzies you may have missed. If you have a fireplace, stoke it up, kill the room lights (and TV, of course), and gather 'round. Tell your own Christmas stories or read some aloud. Sing the carols, make the gingerbread house, bake the cookies, stuff the turkey, shoot your own Christmas card photos, make the eggnog, hang the mistletoe (and keep it away from your kid—the stuff is poison), and kiss Mommy under it. Have your buddy stop by dressed as Santa. And make sure video is rolling.

The beauty of the holidays is best viewed reflected in your child's face. You'll find that like most great trips, the journey trumps the destination. Sure they dig Christmas morning and tearing into the gifts under the tree, but before too long, watch that old ennui set in. Even they know it's just *stuff*.

Try to keep a Zen head about it all. Small kids are chaos machines and will derail even the most carefully laid plans. Try to manage expectations. Let them know that Santa's a busy guy and doesn't always get everything for everybody.

Some people turn holiday commercialism to their advantage and use Santa as a behavioral threat the rest of the year—*Put down the chain saw, Madison; Santa is watching!* But Santa as bogey man has a downside—if he withholds gifts for bad behavior, it's tacitly understood he must bestow them for *good* behavior. Which means you could find yourself duking some clerk at Toys "R" Us a Benjamin so he'll sneak you a copy this year's must-have toy. Remember Cabbage Patch Dolls? Furby toys? Teddy Ruxpins, and Tickle Me Elmos? Do you really want to inculcate junior with the gimme/gotta have mind-set?

If the religious aspect of the holidays is important to you, then you can emphasize Christmas or Chanukah and de-emphasize the gifts. Tell the stories to your kid and let him know that's what it's all about. You can try to position toys as a bonus or secondary benefit (tough to do when Mattel and Hasbro are spending gazillions pitching their wares).

Ultimately, doesn't our lust for stuff fade? Think of that first car, shiny tick-tock or electronic gizmo. Where are they now? It's amazing how, after a brief interval, a car morphs from a sexual obsession to transportation to a bucket of bolts you are eager to unload. If *stuff* is what a kid is taught to value, he'll spend a life-time in pursuit of . . . *stuff*.

A very wise man once said there are only three true necessities in life. A career you like, a nice place to live, and a good love and/or family life. After that, everything else really is just . . . stuff—which winds up worn out, outgrown, or obsolete.

But hey, Scrooge was no one to emulate. And the Christmas spirit is a cool thing that comes but once a year. Why not buy your kid his dream toy? To avoid disappointment, just be sure Santa is listening—carefully. (While you're at it, you may want to inform the sous Santas—Grandma and Grandpa—about the kind of gifts your kid likes. It will save time, money, and the effort of tossing them or hiding them from your child.)

Kids have very particular ideas about what they want in toys. But they can be shy or inaccurate when articulating their desires. Listen closely and if you don't understand, ask questions until you do.

I still recall my disappointment and frustration when, at around age five, I asked Santa for a puppet. I hoped for a big, malev-olent-looking ventriloquist's dummy, with a moving head, jaw, and eyeballs. I had fantasies of throwing my voice and entertaining appreciative hoards with my kooky vaudevillian act. Santa brought me a puppet—sort of. It was the head of Snow White's idiot dwarf, Dopey, with a green fedora and a felt body. No way he was gonna crack wise, not with his missing chromosome expression. Worse, not a damn thing moved—for there was no jaw, no mouth, and nowhere to throw my voice. When no one was looking, I used to put him on my left hand and mercilessly punch his face with my right. I would have been happy with a sock puppet—anything that would have allowed me to make the puppet talk. All Dopey could do was grin like a mute moron.

I remember another Christmas when my older brother, who could tell time, received a Timex. In the interest of fairness, I, too, was given a watch. But mine was a toy—the hands never moved and it didn't tick. Santa knew I couldn't yet tell time, but what made him think I was also deaf and blind? Bad move, Santa.

What kinds of toys to buy? Real toys—that is, things that can actually be *played* with—(folks in the biz call these *open-end play* toys) are best. This eliminates stuffed toys—okay for a week-old infant, but a lousy choice for even a three-month-old with all his buttons. After he hugs it and rubs his face on it, what's it good for? Might as well skin the damn thing and use it to buff the Buick.

Toys are a great way to discover your kid's passions and talents. All kinds of instruments, from percussion to guitars and keyboards come in cheap, kiddie versions that can help you discover whether you've sired a budding Baker, Hendrix, or Joel. Ditto the sports equipment. They've been cranking out Erector Sets for a century, and who knows how many Van der Rohes or Wrights have been inspired by them? They've gotten so good at making them that they have specific sets designed for aviation, automotive, heavy equipment, boats—it's fantastic—and they rank them by skill level, too. Lincoln Logs and Leggos are cool. Kids love dominos. They're fun to count, fun to stack—hell, maybe a long row of them led Edward Teller to flash on nuclear fission. I recollect a cousin enthralled by a doctor kit she was given around age eight. She drove us nuts plucking our hair and demanding cheek swabs for her microscope. Her old man took note—today she's a medical doctor.

Any toy that can do no more than sit on a shelf and be looked at is a toy not worth house room—unless it's something your kid builds or assembles and *then* puts on a shelf. They make terrific kits for everything, from doll houses to F-16s.

If you have the time and desire, you can skip the kits and DIY. As a bachelor, I had a dinky Nativity set with tiny figurines. When I got married, every year, my wife would groan as we set it out with the other Christmas decorations. I'd say, "I gotta get a new one," but didn't. I procrastinated for a couple of reasons. First, most of the ones in stores are cheesy-looking junk. Want something substantial? You'll have to hunt around and be prepared to lay out $500 or more . . . for $25 worth of lumber. And even at that price, the construction is still second-rate, with particle-board backs.

No doubt my father faced the same dilemma. As a very young kid, I recall a small, flimsy Nativity. By the time I was seven or eight, it had been dumped and I was standing by his side at the workbench, handing him screwdrivers and sanding wood as he crafted a big, deluxe, one-of-a-kind, sturdy-as-a-fort Nativity stable. It was fabulous. Somehow it was lost over the years. I always blamed myself for not guarding it more jealously.

I never realized the second reason for not buying a better stable despite Irene's justified complaint. It was so I could experience the fun of building a Nativity with my own child. Losing my dad's creation was part of the karmic plan. I just didn't see it at the time. You never do.

The Nativity construction occupied many hours. I'm no carpenter, and have only some basic tools. Because of her passion, Olivia didn't even mind the trips to Home Depot. Eventually we built a pretty cool stable. And if it somehow gets lost, that's okay. She'll remember the fun we had and maybe someday build one with her son or daughter.

When selecting toys for your kid, it's okay to be a little selfish, too. They love it when Daddy gets down on the floor and plays with the same toys. So if the toy is something that interests you, too, you'll be more likely to accommodate. There's a website that specializes in cool toys for your kid—www.fatbraintoys.com.

The Joke's on Dad

There's a paucity of gags out there about fatherhood. The few you do hear are the kind of unfunny crap you'd see in *Reader's Digest*. Here are a few good ones.

A teacher asks the class to discuss what their dads do for a living.

Little Emily says, "My daddy is a policeman; he puts bad men in jail."

Little Jason says, "My father's a doctor. He makes sick people better."

Little Johnny has yet to speak. The teacher says, "Johnny, what does your dad do?"

Johnny says, "My dad is dead."

"I'm sorry to hear that. What did he do before he died?"

"He turned blue and shit on the carpet."

"Hey, Grandma, can you make a noise like a frog?"

"I think I can do that. Why?"

" 'Cuz Dad says when you croak, we're going to Disney World."

A dad is driving his five-year-old when another car cuts them off, nearly causing a collision.

"Douchebag!" the father yells. A moment later he realizes the indiscretion, pulls over, and turns to his son. "I just said a bad word," he says. "I was angry at that driver, but that was no excuse for what I said. It was wrong. But just because I said it, it doesn't make it right, and I don't ever want to hear you saying it. Okay?"

His son looks at him and says: "Too late, douchebag."

A father is explaining ethics to his son, who is opening a store.

"Say a woman comes in and orders a hundred dollars' worth of goods. You wrap it up and give it to her. She hands you a $100 bill. But as she's leaving, you realize she's given you two $100 bills. Now, here's where the ethics come in: Should you or should you not tell your partner?"

One day Tommy burst into the house and yelled, "Dad! Mom! I have some great news! I'm getting married to the most beautiful girl. She lives a block away and her name is Jennifer."

Later, Tommy's dad took him aside, "Son, I have to talk with you. Your mother and I have been married 30 years, she's a wonderful wife and mother, but she's never offered much excitement in the bedroom, so I . . . I used to fool around with women a lot. Jennifer is actually your half-sister. You can't marry her."

Tommy was crushed. After a year he started dating again. Soon, he came home and proudly announced, "Audrey said yes! We're getting married in May."

Again his father gave him bad news. "Audrey is your half-sister, too. I'm really sorry."

Tommy was furious. He decided to go to his mother with his father's revelations.

"I guess I'm never going to get married," he complained. "Every time I fall in love, Dad tells me the girl is my half-sister."

"Heh-heh," his mother chuckled. "Don't pay any attention to what he says. He's not really your father."

Chapter 8

School

Fighting the Contagion Your Kid (and You) Will Bring Home

People have all kinds of weird ideas about babies. It seems the most common misperception is that they have the constitution of a smoke ring.

The Korean apple guy at the farmer's market would shake his head when he'd see the baby uncovered in a stroller, on a sunny day in the mid-70s. "Yoo bedda covuh dat baby up . . . iss *cole* tooday!" he'd warn. A couple from Belarus said we were nuts to take our three-week-old outside on a windy day for fear of . . . they couldn't say exactly, it just *wasn't a good thing to do.*

Your baby's only a week old? What are you doing outside with it? This was the most common admonishment. You take the baby outside when you bring it home from the hospital. And when you bring it to the pediatrician. What's the big danger? Hospitals are germ farms—airborne contagion is everywhere. Compared to the interior of a hospital, the great outdoors is practically sterile.

When's the last time someone with a communicable/fatal disease stayed at *your* house? The faster you get your kid home from the hospital, the safer he'll be.

Some baby manuals insist you *boil everything!* So, first time around, we boiled all the nipples, collars, and bottles, as if our kitchen were an Ebola hot zone. But think about it . . . that baby's hands touch things—a wall, the arm of a chair, the changing table, *your* hands . . . have all those things been boiled? It's nutty. So for the second baby, nipples, collars, and bottles went in the dishwasher. No illness. No problem.

Doctors say babies are born with amped-up immune systems. If they get breast-fed, that helps maintain the strong levels. We found this to be true when about three months into our second daughter's life, Mommy, Big Sister, and Daddy all caught raging colds and spent several days spraying our home with infected sputum. Guess who didn't catch that cold?

There are some things you can do to lessen the contagion in your home. First, wash those hands. Think of all the human bacterial bombs you shake hands with in a typical business day—those dirty birds that take a leak, dump, and then head back to the office—or the commissary or restaurant, with nary a glance at the sink or soap. In my suit days, I witnessed more than one corporate titan head for the crapper with the *Wall Street Journal* under one arm and a sandwich in the other. *Great place for a snack, boss!*

When your toddler gets home from school, make him wash his hands first. Take a tip from the Japanese—kick off those Bruno Maglis the moment you enter the house. Think of all the nifty places the soles of those shoes have been today . . . marinating in other guys' piss as you stood at the urinal . . . at the Chevron station, standing on a so-fresh-it's-still-jiggling oyster hocked up by a tuberculin wino mere seconds before your arrival. Then, it's "Hi, honey, I'm home!" and you stroll around the house, the soles of those shoes now festering petri dishes of disease, spreading microscopic crawlies around the cut-piles and Karastans on which your five-month-old will creep, roll, and slobber.

No kid or adult should ever use handkerchiefs. They are for the jacket pockets of fops and funeral directors. Anyone who actually uses one as he would a Kleenex needs his head examined. I love watching handkerchief users in action. *Aaaahhhhh-CHOO!* Then, into fine Irish linen, they blow enough ropey green goo to fill a Mason jar. Real pros make a double-decker mucus sandwich by layering the nasal snot with some coughed-up lugers. Then they take a good gander at it all, presumably to be sure it doesn't contain any misplaced Dodger tickets, jewelry, or key fobs. Next, they fold it neatly and place it in their pocket, a precious keepsake to have, hold, and treasure. Why don't they wrap their *shit* in linen and pocket that, too?

After the hand washing and shoe removal, it's just a common-sense checklist of stuff to do. Every so often, wipe the crib rails—the one where baby likes to teethe—with disinfectant. If he spits the pacifier onto the ground, keep it from him until you can wash it. If you hear there's been an outbreak of cholera at nursery school, let the kids stay home and watch *SpongeBob*.

Most annoying of all are the parents who regard nursery school as an infirmary and blithely send their medicated but still-contagious whooping coughing/strep-throated kids off to school because it's *convenient for them*. These are usually the same yo-yos that pride themselves on their flawless attendance records at work, and show up regardless of their communicable ailments. These selfish, inconsiderate, ignorant mommies and daddies should be horsewhipped . . . in public.

Bad Company, Bullies, and Bitches

You make a baby and try to do everything right. You build up his ego, give him a sense of honor, and fair play. Doing this all involves a number of white lies. *That drawing is beautiful! You sing like an angel. Yes, that throw went at least a mile. No, I couldn't ride a two-wheeler until I was twice your age. Yes, Mommy was my first and only girlfriend.*

Once you take your child to school, all that can be undone in a matter of minutes by rotten, nasty kids.

Do you know any pricks? A guy who should be bitch-slapped so hard, his teeth fly out of his mouth? Well, what do you think that guy was like as a child?

Are some kids just born evil? Could be. Why was Jeffrey Dahmer torturing small animals and impaling their severed heads on spikes around his house as a boy? Most awful adults started as awful kids.

In grammar school, there were a couple of punks in my older brother's class. They were legendary hoodlums. One guy, by age 9, was characterized by a nun as "already in hell." (Most of us attending that school felt we were in hell, too, but Sister Paul had a point.) His name was Gary, and his face was a portrait of madness. At 11 years of age, he and his pal Vinny were arrested for molesting a little girl at knife-point. By the time they were graduating (grammar school, mind you), rumors of Gary and Vinnie's burglaries, car thefts, and heroin use abounded—odds are, they were all true.

Our parents ordered us to avoid these two creeps at all costs, and we did.

Years later, I bumped into a guy from the old neighborhood. "Whatever happened to those two stone psychos, Gary and Vinnie?"

His answer was not unexpected. Gary became a mainlining junkie, and one night drove his mother and sister into a canal, drowning all three. Vinnie left this world in an even more spectacular fashion. He was dealing huge quantities of drugs. When they came to get him, he took his own kid hostage and held off a squad of New York's Finest for several hours. Finally, he released the kid and kicked open the front door, guns blazing. The cops filled him with enough lead to sink a barge.

Thankfully, there aren't too many Garys and Vinnies around. But your child may encounter one or two as he matriculates. How do you handle it?

Don't sugar-coat your appraisal of the kid. The nun was dead right. So were my parents, who, in plain terms, explained that kids like Gary and Vinnie ended up in jail or dead, and those who hung around with them often shared their fate. So much for bad company.

Bullies are invariably cowards wrapped in bravado. If your son is being bullied, you can try to handle it for him, but that sets an awful precedent. You can go to the teacher, but that teacher cannot watch your kid constantly. You could grab the kid's father and talk to him, but he's probably the asshole with the bumper sticker on his F-150 that says, *My kid can kick your honor student's ass.* Sooner or later, a determined bully will get your boy alone. Then what?

The instant your son complains of bullying, immediately enroll him in a school for self-defense—even if you have to sell blood to pay for it. Avoid traditional dojos with all the protracted programs, the katas, bowing, and sensei bullshit. Most of these "sport" martial arts academies produce "dojo darlings" with just enough confidence to get their asses kicked by a good street fighter. Their "tournaments" and "competitions" are in controlled, supervised environments. Your six-year-old's encounter with a bully will be unscheduled, unsupervised, and unpleasant. He needs quick results.

There are now many martial arts schools that cut to the chase— teaching your kid to knock some bully on his ass, and if he gets up, to knock him down again. Krav Maga, the hand-to-hand combat system of Israeli armed forces, gets high marks and is taught around the country. Then there's American Combat Karate, which cherry picks the best techniques from boxing, grappling, and Asian martial arts. There are several others.

If Mom disagrees with the self-defense solution, tell her she's out of her range of experience. Period.

Violence is traumatic. It's a negative, life-altering occurrence. Most males, by adulthood, have sustained a fist to the face, a kick in the balls, a fat lip, or a blackened eye. Few females have had these experiences. That's why their take on violence is usually flawed. *Hug him. Reason with him. Show him love. Violence begets violence* . . . only until you knock the other bastard unconscious.

What if your kid is the aggressor? That can be even tougher. He needs to be shown the error of his ways or some other kid (perhaps one whose old man has enrolled his son in martial arts classes) will teach him a lesson. If your son is bullying people, this is usually indicative of some other psychological issues. Is there a problem at home? Maybe you all need a therapist.

Girls have their own brand of aggression—one that better equips them for battle in politics, corporations, and the allegedly "civilized" world.

A recent study from Brigham Young University found that girls as young as three or four will use manipulation and peer pressure to get what they want. Methods include leaving someone out from play, telling Jennifer and Emily not to play with "that bitch Madison," or the tried-and-true "I'm not gonna invite you to my birthday party." As a last resort, there's always, "I won't be your friend."

Who needed the Brigham Young study? Anyone raising a girl has seen this nonsense up close. I wonder if the Brigham Young team encountered suburban preschool girls giving each other bags of shit about their weight, tan lines, and clothing designers, because I've seen all that in L.A. It's horrific.

The only way to shield them from this stuff is with home schooling. If they go to school, you have to ground their values early and armor-plate their egos. Don't let them participate in acquisitive one-upsmanship. That's a sucker's walk and a sure-fire way to raise an empty, unhappy child. There's always a richer, crazier parent who will buy their brat a bigger, better Vuitton lunch box, Rolex, or Donzi.

The best way to combat the "gimmes" is by cultivating your child's talents, whatever they may be. Whether it's music, dance, sports, art, math, sewing, carpentry—whatever will give her a sense of accomplishment will help keep her immune not only to the pressures of kid consumerism, but to the slings and arrows classmates may throw at her.

Making Sure Your Child Digs School

School. Now *there's* a loaded word, with as many different meanings as the people you ask about it. I recently learned an old friend's high school experience was absolute hell. He was small, bookish, shy, and had no friends. We met as adults, and I had no idea.

I recall well my own grammar school experience in NYC. The building was ancient. The dark, dank hallways still had capped gas jets—a vestige of the days before electricity. The stairs had endured so many scuffing shoes over the decades that the marble steps were deeply warped. The place smelled of disinfectant and was run like a prison by some pretty brutal Dominican nuns. There was nothing warm and fuzzy about them—the first priority was discipline, next came learning. For some reason, they all had *men's* names—Sister Paul Gerard, Sister James Bernard, Sister John Wayne, Sister Warren Oates.

There were few smiles, no hugs, and if you got out of line, those beefy penguins wouldn't hesitate to twist your ear, pull your hair, smack a ruler across your knuckles, or leave a red hand print on your cheek. (Funny, they never blushed when reading the Gospel passage about *turn the other cheek*. On the other hand, they probably got a thrill over *suffer the little children*.)

To me, grammar school was primarily a place of fear and suffering. Hopefully, such places have become rare on American soil.

School Caveats

A MACK DADDY has already screened the faculty and grounds and found everything acceptable, but there are still a plethora of x-factors to contend with. How your kid will adapt to and perform at school (and in life, for that matter) depends upon his or her ego. Is it Kevlar or Kleenex? That will largely depend on *you*.

Remember, kids are little people who've yet to learn to lie socially. If a child is overweight, he *will* be called fat. If he's clumsy, sloppy, has bad breath, or farts a lot, ALL of these attributes will be noted, amplified, and harped on by his class-mates. How to prepare him for these trials? First, he and especially *she* should *not* be fat. If he or she is, it's the parents' fault. Sure, some kids are genetically programmed to be short, tall, wiry, or thick. But obesity is a function of diet and anyone who thinks otherwise is delusional.

You see parents everywhere force-feeding their kids. Then when they become obese, it's *Oh, little Bobby has big bones!* Or, *Christina has a slow metabolism.* But the kids in school ain't buying into their parental spin. They're calling them 'em *Blobby* and *Tubby Tina*, with the added descriptors *lard-ass and jelly-belly.*

Of course, some equally deluded educators think they can eradicate cruelty, taunting, and teasing. They can—and should—in the classroom. But what about in the schoolyard, on the bus, or walking home? What then? Will each kid get his own faculty ego-guard to ensure he doesn't sustain any emotional bruising? If that were possible, who would protect him when he's alone and looks in the mirror?

The "Fat's Okay" lobby insists that fat is fine, it's the average bodyweight people who need to adjust their attitudes. If fat is fine, why do the doctors and actuaries tell us fat is fatal?

Obesity is an avoidable tragedy. Two-year-olds can't pop the fridge, slap together a Dagwood, and garnish it with a dozen Ding Dongs. Somebody has to put that food in front of him or her. This is one of the few areas where parents are in complete control of the situation and can raise either a normal kid or an obese one.

Kids will latch on to anything different and make fun of it. It's up to the parent to prep the kid. I was a redhead. When I came home and told Mom and Dad they called me "carrot top," Mom said, "Well aren't they stupid! Carrot tops are green." Bang. I had my snappy comeback. When I was seven, I had a "lazy" eye which necessitated that I wear an eye patch. Knowing the flack I'd be getting, my old man—a world-class MACK DADDY—said, "Tell 'em you're a pirate—and say it like you mean it." The last phrase he put in the face/voice of a rummed-up Blackbeard. When I hit the classroom, I was bulletproof, and after the initial *one-eye* taunts subsided, some other kids actually started aping the style with their homemade patches.

My older daughter went through an Alice-in-Wonderland phase. A family friend gave her a realistic blond wig, which Olivia would don as she held tea parties. One morning, she headed for nursery school with the wig on. Little girls can be incredibly bitchy and I knew the wig could draw flack. As I drove her to school, I tried to talk her into leaving the wig behind, but she was adamant. So, I prepped her instead, telling her how beautiful she looked and that some girls, being jealous of her wig, might say something mean about it, but not to listen because she was beautiful no matter what.

That evening, I asked her how it went, and she said almost everyone liked her wig. "Who didn't like your wig," I asked.

"Lauren, but she was jealous."

Mission accomplished.

Now, if you have a five-year-old *son* who wants to wear a long blond wig, with purse and shoes that match, you've got a little bit tougher problem. But you can handle that, too.

Never let your kid suffer an ambush. The day my daughter started first grade, all the parents were asked to show up for a few minutes, to meet the teacher and help their kids settle in. One little boy—Shawn—was considerably larger than the other kids. His father stayed only a few seconds and then split. The teacher took attendance and welcomed everyone to first grade. Shawn's hand shot up.

"Excuse me, I have to go," said Shawn.

"Why," asked the teacher.

"There's been a mistake. This is first grade. I'm supposed to be in *second* grade. I went to first grade last year."

The teacher's face reddened. Poor Shawn's chickenshit, ignorant, cruel and irresponsible old man didn't tell his son he was repeating first grade—letting the boy be humiliated and the teacher flummoxed. Thinking about Shawn's dad, I wondered which archetype he fit—Distant, Lactating, Rubber-Stamp or Der Fuehrer. He earned his own category—asshole.

The only surprises kids really like are the ones that are gift wrapped. Be kind—give a heads-up about anything that may rock his world.

Hitler: A *Zero Tolerance* Kinda Guy

One of the most daunting challenges facing dads is getting their kid educated. And it's not just a matter of tuition—it's making sure your child is being educated, not *indoctrinated*. If the school's curriculum fits your own views, or the ones you'd like your kid exposed to, fine. It's a good idea to find out in advance.

Look at the books, talk to the teachers, ask to audit a class. It won't take long to suss out what they're all about. Remember, there is no such thing as an objective opinion. Everybody's going to put their spin on history, science, and the like.

With religious schools, you won't need to do much detective work; their agendas are usually right out front. But still, you should ask the tough questions—what is their policy regarding such subjects as sex-ed, apparel, homework, lateness, and discipline. Better to get it in advance from the faculty than to have your six-year-old surprise you with his sudden and thorough knowledge of human reproduction.

All the above is applicable only if you have a *choice* in where you send your child to school. Many people don't, due to financial or geographic reasons. In this case, you may be facing quite a dilemma.

Right from kindergarten, many schools teach with a bias that pushes their point of view. Of course, they'll never admit it. You have to look for the red flags. You'll find a flapping, crimson one in these two words: **zero tolerance.** When spoken in earnest, here is what they say about the speaker: *I'm a well-educated moron. I really don't like kids. I'm a social pariah and want to make your kid one, too. I'm weak and powerless, but within the confines of this school, I am powerful and enjoy exerting my authority over your children. When I see newsreel footage of goose-stepping Nazis, I become sexually aroused. I lack the judgment to make intelligent decisions, therefore I mindlessly spew "policy."*

Zero tolerance people are a lot like message T-shirt (and bumper-sticker) people. What do their T-shirts say, regardless of what's written on them? This: *I don't have anything remotely intelligent to say, so until I do, just read my shirt.*

The zero tolerance stories are legion, and they continue to flow as the cultural Marxists' stranglehold tightens on our schools. If you've not heard any, here are some classics: The ten-year-old girl who asked a boy if he "liked her" and was suspended for violating the zero tolerance sexual harassment policy. A seven-year-old who, after forming his hand in the shape of a pistol and pointing it at another kid, was suspended from a Connecticut school for making a *terrorist threat.* A number of kids have been thrown out of schools for taking aspirin, in violation of zero tolerance drug policies. Kids have been bounced because they possessed *cough* drops. The kid in Oregon who was banned from posting a photograph of her bother the Marine, because in it, he held a rifle—violating the school's zero tolerance for weapons.

What we need is zero tolerance for zero tolerance people. They are sometimes fascists, often elitist, invariably stupid and dangerous.

Zero tolerance proponents both terrorize and criminalize our children, and then once accused, deny them due process. They piss on our Constitution. Zero tolerance is really about power, and making school administrators into dictators, enabling them to declare a photograph a *weapon*, a cough drop a *drug* or an innocent question, *sexual harassment*.

I guarantee you, as a dad, you will endure more nonsense and hassles from your children than you could possibly imagine. And because you are a MACK DADDY, you will be, above all else, *tolerant*. These are school children; not convicts. If our children don't deserve our tolerance, who does?

Now for the good news. Schools are not the federal government. You can *sue* them. If your child is a victim of zero tolerance/ fascist garbage masquerading as "educators," run to your attorney. This is still America, and anybody attempting to criminalize your kid should be sued into destitution.

If your only local educational option is a hot-bed of zero toler-ance you may want to consider home schooling. With public schools in a shambles and private ones priced to bankrupt, over 1.5 million U.S. kids are being home schooled. It's legal in all 50 states but each varies as to requirements and standards to be met.

Proponents claim excellent results, with significantly higher SAT scores. Opponents (including the National Parent Teacher Association, no surprise there, huh?) say home schooling denies kids "socialization." But, home schoolers often do so in concert with other local families and arrange for plenty of exposure to other kids.

The benefits or drawbacks of home schooling ultimately depend on the parents. Not everyone is cut out to be a teacher. It takes incredible patience, and a genuine love for kids and imparting knowledge to them. Teachers are among the most underpaid, overworked professionals in the nation. And most of them are wonderful. But not those zero tolerance imbeciles.

When They're Out to Get Your Kid

Like the old line goes, "Just because we're paranoid, it doesn't mean they're not out to get us."

Kids of either sex come with their own set of difficulties. And both can be as different as day and night. No question, little girls can be manipulative, sneaky drama queens. But it's the boys who are more likely to create situations that land you in faculty conference rooms.

Some interesting stats just emerged that I, a father of two girls, never thought about. Believe it or not, a pretty hefty number of kids each year get expelled from . . . *nursery school*. How can this be? What could a three-, four-, or five-year-old child possibly do that warrants expulsion? According to the stats, kids in preschool are expelled at 3 times the rate of older kids. The Yale Child Study Center found that 7 out of 1,000 preschool kids are being expelled, compared with 2 per 1,000 elementary, middle and high school students. And of those expelled, boys are being thrown out at 4.5 times the rate of girls. (No surprise there.) What if *your* boy gets bounced?

Who is doing the teaching, particularly in the lower grades? Overwhelmingly, women. Some are quite adept at dealing with young boys who are, by nature, more manic, spirited, and aggressive than girls. Some are not so adept. Perhaps themselves raised by a single mom, they may have no idea how to deal with young boys. There's really nothing new here—remember Mom yelling at her disobedient sons, "Wait till your father gets home."

Since time immemorial, Dad was considered the household sheriff. But now, Dad's been emasculated, leaving a terrible void in the home and the classroom. Who has the authority, the *command presence* as they say in the military, to kick ass and take names?

So what do these preschools do? They wig out, branding the boy a disciplinary problem, who is *disruptive* and *acts out.* That may be the perception, but what's likely the reality? He's a *boy,* that's what! And boys are, by and large, not hard-wired (as girls are) to sit nicely for hours on end and pay attention.

What's their remedy? One easy out is to build a case and have him expelled. If you get a whiff of that from a teacher, you have a couple of plays. If you really, really need this school for your kid, *do not* engage the faculty in verbal combat. They would love nothing more than to label you "abusive" and "uncooperative," just like your son.

Instead, take a page from the masters of corporate judo. When incompetent execs first scent the stench of failure around them for some deal they've screwed-up to a fare-thee-well, what do they do? Amateurs try to bury it. (Never works.) Devious pricks try to lay the blame on subordinates. (Sometimes works.) But the clever, "fail-upward" experts sound a general alarm (with a blizzard of memos) and enlist the help of their superiors. Soon, *their* problem becomes *everyone's* problem and when the shit flies, *everyone* gets spattered. So sometimes, the problem is fixed or more often, the problem is declared no longer a problem and it goes away.

When you first catch a drift that they want to sack your kid, immediately knock out a letter to the teacher and copy the principal. Thank them for bringing your son's *situation* or *difficulty* (never problem or condition) to your attention and say how you look forward to *working with* them to get the *assistance* he needs to restore him to academic excellence, blah blah bullshit bullshit. If the principal has a brain in her skull, she'll realize she's not dealing with a piker and either back off your kid or get him the extra attention he needs.

If she doesn't, you should prominently copy your attorney on the next letter. I guarantee this will at least buy you some time to find another school or work it through with your son.

Remember, it's a nasty game, and the pawn is your little boy. The faculty's been through it before, but not with a kid whose old man is a MACK DADDY. Keep your cool, use your head, and you can leave your footprints on their asses.

Just Say No (Particularly to the Drugs They Try to Shove Down His Throat)

Another option they may offer is drugs. Our idiotic War on Drugs has spanned five decades. There's no end in sight and we're farther from victory than at its declaration, yet our schools are pushing a drug the DEA designates as Class II—same as morphine and barbiturates. It's called Ritalin, and if some "educator" suggests it for your allegedly ADHD-afflicted, *disruptive* son, beware!

Some estimates place the number of Ritalin-"medicated" boys at 4 million. Why such a vast number? Nobody seems to have a good answer.

Ritalin side effects include depression, lethargy, and social withdrawal. With prolonged use, Ritalin can generate the very symptoms it is supposed to quell—hyperactivity, bad temper, and inability to concentrate. Quite the wonder drug, eh?

Odds are, your kid does not need any drugs whatsoever. It's likely certain substances and stimuli are creating or aggravating his condition. Cut the sweets—they hit kids like amphetamines. Be sure he's not ingesting any caffeine—it's not just in Coke, coffee, and Red Bull, it's in most chocolate, too. Cut out the TV/video games. They torque up his brain. Make sure he's getting enough sleep and double his exercise to dissipate more of that nervous energy. Try teaching him some yoga and deep breathing/relaxation, too. Try to find out what other shit is going on that might make him jinky. Is he being bullied? Ridiculed? Is he getting enough attention from his mom, and especially, his dad?

PC Educational Glossary

Once your child starts school, you will be assaulted with a barrage of euphemisms and politically correct verbiage. Nobody wants their kid to be another brick in the wall and everybody's kid must be *special* (result: no one is special). In service to these concepts, teachers have developed their own lingua franca which you must learn.

Your child is bright.   He's an imbecile. (Average kids are now called brilliant.)

Your child plays well alone.   He's a pariah.

Your child is very active.   They'll be recommending he go on Ritalin.

Your child is strong-willed.   He's an obnoxious brat. They'll be recommending Ritalin.

Your child needs to address some socialization issues.   He laid another kid out cold with a folding chair to the head.

Your child is very sweet.   He has the personality of a boulder.

Are there some problems at home?   That squirrel-head impaled on the fence post was put there by your kid.

You child certainly is verbal.   She called the teacher a *fuckin' ho.*

Kid as Public Enemy

Der Fuehrer Daddies aren't necessarily of Teutonic heritage. I saw one in action who had a thick Irish brogue. I was in a playground and there were these cute little plastic animals—a seal, a pony, and a tiger mounted on leaf springs—just the right size for kids from about three to six. I was sitting on a bench with Olivia. Along came this dad with a cute little red haired boy of about three or four. He made a bee line for the one unoccupied animal, the seal. Simultaneously, another little boy headed for the seal.

The redhead was a little quicker and hopped aboard. No big deal, there were several animals and kids got on and off them quickly.

Suddenly, I heard a shrieking voice.

"DERMOT! GET OFF THAT RIDE AND LEAVE IT TO THAT CHILD!"

Dermot leapt off the plastic seal like it was a sizzling griddle. But, the other boy whom he'd beaten out did not mount up. He just stood in slack-jawed amazement, as did everyone in the park, at the insane outburst by Dermot's old man.

And I'm thinking . . . *Is Dermot a midget? That other little boy is about the same age—is he here from the Make a Wish Foundation or something?*

At the sound of his old man's voice, Dermot obeyed and then stood silently, head bowed and shoulders hunched in a pose of shame.

Anybody want to place any bets on how Dermot's life will turn out? From which drive-thru window will Dermot's handsome adult head pop hundreds of thousands of times in his lifetime fast food career because his old man told him he was lower than whale shit?

Der Fuehrer Dad's Antithisis: Permissive Pop

Now the flip side is the horrifically permissive parent, who also usually thinks his kid has the right to knock Dermot off the plastic seal.

One hundred eighty degrees from Dermot's old man is Permissive Daddy. I saw one of these guys in action at a movie theater. His five- or six-year-old boy was running up and down the aisles. Then, he'd run through empty rows shouting and singing. This went on for 15 or 20 minutes. (This was not a matinee.) The brat ran through an empty row, slapping the backs of the heads of audience members. I was half expecting Ashton and his *Punk'd* crew to appear. Suddenly a guy whose head was slapped sprung to his feet and bellowed, "Who owns that little bastard?"

Little Bastard's father stood up, "That's my son Jason, and who the hell are you to call him a bastard?"

On screen, Angelina Jolie could have been giving head to a Cape buffalo and no one would have looked. Every eye was riveted on the combatants.

"I'm the guy that Jason's gonna watch kick your ass, if you don't get him under control, that's who."

That pretty much settled it.

Jason's daddy grabbed him and hauled ass out of the theater amid riotous applause.

Somewhere between Dermot's old man and Jason's, you'll find MACK DADDIES. It's okay to let a kid be a kid, but there's a time and place for everything.

How about the kid who spends a transcontinental flight kicking your seat back? His old man's right next to him, fully reclining his seat into the guy's lap behind *him*.

Or the little bastard in the restaurant booth behind you who thinks the seat is a trampoline?

It's so clear. The reason we have ignorant people is ignorant parents.

Chapter 9

Cutting Yourself Some Slack

MACK DADDIES have a high standard to live up to. They're a cut above. But while you're doing the best you can, don't forget to cut yourself some slack. You are a flesh and blood dad. You put up with shit at work, with traffic, with dozens of other daily annoyances. Sometimes, you'll be under incredible pressure. Your toddler will whine or spread peanut butter on your computer keyboard or throw darts at your plasma TV and *ker-plow,* you blow. Every dad does it, any who denies it is lying or insane. You'll get frustrated and mad and yell at your child, and maybe with considerably more volume and anger than warranted. Then, you'll feel like shit.

You won't get to attend every one of your child's ball games or piano recitals. You'll blow off the pony ride you promised her or glance at her latest drawing, say a hurried and inadequate 'yeah, that's great,' see the disappointment on her face and feel like stabbing yourself in the skull.

Your kid will challenge you, you'll forget all your mental judo and instead of finessing him from the bathtub, you'll bodily haul him out, kicking and screaming. When caught in the crossfire of whines, demands, and flying toys, you *will* snap and bellow SHUT UP!

These things will happen. One of the amazingly wonderful things about kids is, they quickly forget and tend not to hold grudges. Don't hold one against yourself.

Situations Your Kid Puts You In

It takes 10 years to become a Zen priest. A 10th Dan Black Belt in Judo can take 35 or 40 years. You can father a child in a matter of minutes. Raising one takes a lifetime.

Over time, you'll just be amazed at the situations you can find yourself in, thanks to your kid. How does this happen? Well, as a MACK DADDY, from the moment you lay eyes on your son or daughter, you will gladly donate a kidney, eye, or bone marrow, or take a bullet for that child.

There are guys whose idea of roughing it is a penthouse suite at the Ritz. And these same guys will hunker down for a weekend in a mosquito-infested pup tent with their 11-year-old Boy Scout son because . . . it's his *son*.

So, get ready for the sacrifice. That's what a true MACK DADDY is all about. It's not about scrimping to get your kid what he needs. (And if you do, Bravo, baby!) MACK DADDIES can be whales, but still, they *sacrifice*.

By nursery school time, you'll find yourself in all kinds of kook-azoid situations you never ever could have imagined. You'll be having forced interface with parents who seem like they just surfed in on the rings of Saturn.

Case in point: Somebody says to a MACK DADDY friend of mine, "Hey, I'll pick up your kid from school today, okay?"

This is a nice, generous offer. Hard to imagine it generating some nasty blowback, but it did. En route, some hostile vibe percolates between the kiddies that escalates into fist city. Now, bear in mind, these are five-year-olds. No big deal (unless you're a *zero tolerance* pussy, in which case you call out the National Guard to restore order).

However, while my pal *is* a MACK DADDY, the other daddy is a Lactating Daddy. When he drops off his daughter (yes, girls like violence, too) LD says, *I don't know who started it, but, my Madison tends to be verbal and nonviolent.* What a Lactating Daddy thing to say. Who gives a shit who started it? There were no missing teeth, blackened eyes, or bloody lips—just a couple of little girls cat fighting. But, this is the kind of nonsense you're in for.

There will be parties. And if you are a MACK DADDY, you don't invite your child's entire school, you invite the kids from her class she *wants to invite*. Prepare for the shit storm Monday morning. We received several angry calls from pin-headed parents out-raged at our "exclusionary policies." I wonder if these same people, upon learning their kids aren't admitted to Harvard/Yale/MIT, will be calling those institutions to bitch about their "exclusionary policies?"

Some parents, instead of finding the endless humor in the honesty of children, will take umbrage at the things your child says. A friend of ours got an angry call from a parent who was offended because her child admitted that she was forbidden play dates at so and so's house because they watch R-rated movies—with the kids. This friend took a diplomatic (albeit cowardly) way out, denying the whole situation

No matter how gentle and sweet, your kid will sometimes be a lightning rod for controversy and trouble. And rarely, if ever, will the true source of the problem be a child. It will be that child's idiotic parent.

Bottom line, a MACK DADDY knows when to let stupid behav-ior slide and when to stick to his guns and kick ass. When these silly incidents arise, let this be your primary criterion: was your kid injured, damaged or imperiled by what happened?

In the case of who started the fight, let Lactating Daddy paint a halo over Madison's head and find somebody else to drive your kid. Ditto the party fallout. It's your house and your kid's party and your right to decide who attends. Period.

In the case of the R-rated movie play date, hell yeah, stand your ground. That kid's parents were 100 percent in the wrong. When someone invites your kid into their house, they assume the responsibility for that kid's safety and welfare, and have no right to impose their bizarre tastes in kiddie-tainment. A MACK DADDY would say, *Well yeah, I do have a problem with five-year-olds watching R-rated flicks. Why don't you?*

Don't ever be embarrassed to protect your child. If a classmate invites your kid over for a play date and you're unfamiliar with the parents, make sure you go into the house, hang around, chitchat and scope things out. Do you feel 100 percent comfortable leaving your kid? If not, grab your kid and bolt. Don't sweat the excuses or the fact that your kid will loathe you for a few minutes (or hours). Trust your instincts.

Quality Time

If you think about it on the grand scale, *any* time with your kid should be quality time, because you don't get very much time with your kid. If you extrapolate the total number of hours you'll spend with your child after factoring in work, sleep, commuting, business trips, school, and other distractions—it isn't very much at all.

If a guy is clever, he can make quality time just about anytime he's with his kid. Sounds simple, but it's not always easy. You have to *engage* your kid. When you're driving somewhere and he's in the backseat, kill the radio and talk with him. Or play games with him. Little kids love to play I Spy, where you say *I see something yellow,* and then he has to spot it, whether it's another car, a billboard, or a yield sign. (You don't have to mention it's the leather micro-mini on the babe at the bus stop.) You could count white lines or look for other motorists picking their noses or women with harlequin glasses or bumper stickers. But if you sit there listening to Coldplay or some talk-radio windbag, your kid's a prisoner back there, bored out of his little skull.

If you're digging some tunes, choose some that he can sing along with. If you think back, you may remember what it was like to be a small child. Very often tots, when surrounded by adults, feel alienated. They can't read, and much of adult conversation is over their heads.

Don't most people like to be a part of things? To feel needed and helpful? We can give kids that feeling, even when we're doing all the crappy chores that are a part of life. When you mow the lawn, give your tot a small rake and let her help clean up. Washing the car? An extra sponge for her slop over the car will make her feel great. Give your kid a rag and let him dust the furniture. Vastly preferable to plopping him in front of the tube while you go about your business.

Think about the way the last five or ten years of your life have whizzed by. Before you know it, your toddler will be a teenager, leaping into some other kid's car, heading for God knows where—without you. Can you imagine the feeling in your belly when you witness that?

So, when you can, take your kid along—to Home Depot, to the gas station, for the evening walk, wherever and whenever you can. Bask in the near unconditional worship he or she has for you. It will not last.

MACK DADDY in a Dangerous World

It's inarguable—the world is a more perilous sphere than it used to be. Regardless of catch phrases like *co-parenting, house-husband, stay-at-home dad* and where you may or may not fit into them, know this truth: when apocalyptic shit flies, your wife and kids will be looking to Daddy for salvation. It doesn't matter if she's the breadwinner and he's still trying to get his acting/sculpture/business off the ground. When scary, life-threatening events take place, Daddy must protect and provide. That's your most basic, primordial role—it's not changing, and it never will.

Some wise man once said, "Civilization is never more than three meals from anarchy." Witness New Orleans, post–hurricane Katrina. Victims couldn't dial 911—the phones were dead. Had the phones worked, no one would have answered, because there was mass desertion by the police. In a matter of hours, gangs of armed thugs were looting, robbing, and killing. (They actually shot at the few remaining police and rescue workers.) Even within the "safe haven" of the Superdome, there were several rapes and murders—in a crowd of more than 20,000 people.

New Orleans was hardly an anomaly. In only a two-year span, Los Angeles was twice plunged into prolonged states of near-anarchy. During the '92 riots, police spokesmen told citizens: "911 response times are a minimum six hours—so folks, you're on your own." After the '94 earthquake, I and millions of my neighbors had no water, power, or gas for several days. Police and fire responses were glacial.

Does anyone doubt Al Qaeda will attempt a reprise of 9/11?

Our relatively easy, safe, orderly world is extremely fragile. The weather, an unpopular verdict, or terrorists can instantly knock a modern metropolis into the Stone Age.

Those survivalist guys with their camo ensembles and army surplus inventory don't look so goofy anymore, do they? You don't have to trade your cashmere V-necks for fatigues just yet, but only a moron (or a Lactating or Rubber-Stamp Daddy) wouldn't take some simple measures to ensure he and his family can ride out man-made or natural catastrophes.

Here's the list of things to consider. Whether you're in a high-risk flood/tsunami area, earthquake, brush fire or tornado country, how fast can you get out? Always keep the car fuel tanks at least half full. Get a couple of plastic five-gallon gas cans and keep them in the garage—but remember to switch it out—gas degrades over time—it absorbs water, oxidizes and gets gummy. It has a shelf life of only 6–12 months—less in hot weather. If you run stale gas it will clog fuel injectors, play hell with your motor and crater your evacuation plan.

If disaster strikes and you're staying put, how long can you hold out with no access to water, power or a supermarket? Most important item—water. Keep at least 20 gallons of bottled water around (preferably cool and dark) and freshen that every 18 to 24 months. Have enough canned foods to fill everyone's belly for at least a week. Buy tuna, beans, Spam—stuff you don't have to cook because you may not be able to. Have candles, matches, four or five flashlights, plenty of batteries, and some kind of battery-operated table lamp. Propane lamps are great—they'll brightly light a room for many hours and throw significant heat. Additional propane tanks are only a couple of bucks a pop.

Have a battery-operated radio. You can buy a portable CB radio for $50—could be a lifesaver in an evacuation or catastrophic situation. Have a fully stocked first-aid kit in the home and car trunks.

Armageddonwithit-type dudes with a serious disaster preparedness plan will want a portable power generator. Many companies manufacture them, from Coleman to Honda. A no-name brand that generates around 4,000 watts at peak will cost about $300. Use with care and read instruction manuals like your life depended on it. They're not toys and can be very hazardous.

There's a small but growing crowd attempting to "live off the grid"—the "grid" being the trappings of civilization we're all so dependent upon—tap water, electric power, fire departments, police, and big oil. These guys, if desert rats, generate solar power. If they live near a reliable stream, it's hydroelectric. Some do it in high style, building near palatial digs that are virtually self-sufficient. What's fascinating is the change in their motivation. It's shifted from desire to disconnect to a need to be ready when the grid fails.

What about protection? If you're thinking of getting a firearm for apocalyptic scenarios, a handgun is better than a rifle or shotgun—more easily concealed and stored. Two just-won't-jam, never-fail classics are the Browning Hi-Power 9mm and Smith & Wesson revolvers. Most guns are equally accurate—it's reliability that separates the good from the junk. The two most important factors are your ability to fire it and (for semi-automatics) will it fire without jamming? Some very expensive pistols are surprisingly prone to jamming—which renders them nothing more than pricey paper weights. Most target ranges have a selection you can rent and shoot before you buy.

If you're buying used, have a gunsmith look it over for you. A stainless steel finish may look new, but guns have many moving parts that cannot be seen unless disassembled. A bright, shiny roscoe might be shot out and ready for the slag heap.

Of course, guns and young kids don't mix, but there are many gun safes that are absolutely foolproof. They can be a quarter-ton, refrigerator-sized and secure a small arsenal, or little enough to bolt under a bed, with a push-button combination lock that opens in two seconds or less. The NRA offers inexpensive courses in home firearm safety, as well as pistol, rifle, and shotgun handling. They know what they're doing. Take a course before you buy: www.nra.org.

If you haven't enough to worry about and crave more brain-swelling anxiety, log on to www.survivalist.com. They alphabetize end-of-days scenarios from asteroids to pestilence to volcanoes, providing myriad links for more *good-bye world* despair. Read it and weep.

MACK DADDY Exit Strategies

MACK DADDIES, before they are daddies, are devil-may-care thrill seekers of the highest order—Fugu-gobbling, heli-skiing, bull-running, absinthe-swilling maniacs every one. But when a kid enters the picture, priorities shift. Though MACK DADDIES fully intend to dance at their grandchildren's weddings, they don't always make it.

Once you become a dad, you really need to get your affairs in order.

First order of priority—a will. Sure, you can download a do-it-yourself, legally binding last will and testament—but don't. Get an attorney—a good one—preferably one at least 50 years old. Why? Because he'll have seen or heard of every conceivable contingency that you've yet to imagine.

If you and your wife are immolated in a car crash or pulverized by a rogue meteor, who do you want to raise your kid(s)? Let's say you choose your best friend Lou, a guy you could ask to meet you on a freeway entrance ramp at 2 a.m. with $25k in a gym bag—no questions asked. He'd do it—as you would for him. Is Lou the man? Here's what a slick attorney will ask:

Is Lou married? Does he have kids? How many? How old? Is his marriage stable? Will you leave your assets and/or the kids' college fund in Lou's care?

Then that slick attorney will fire up his crystal ball. Let's see. You're dead 18 years and it's college time for your son. But Lou (or Lou's kid) has a well-hidden gambling jones. He's into bookies and sharks for mid-six figs. He can't make the payment. Guess who's getting your child's college fund? Or maybe Lou's wife has eyes only for her eldest boy, who just *needs* a Ferrari. Watch your kid get downgraded from Stanford to the local junior college.

Now that same attorney, if he's really smart, may suggest you put your money in a trust and have a bank dole it out to Lou as needed. Of course, that may take a little finessing, as Lou's probably thinking, *Hey, that sonafabitch pal of mine croaks and I'm good enough to raise his kid, but I gotta beg some friggin' bank to pay his tuition?*

Lastly, how old is Lou? Ideally, he should be quite a few years younger than you are. If not, he may croak the day after you do and *then* where is your kid?

Parental guardians aside, you don't want your estate plundered by the government. Your state laws may be benign right now, but who knows what greedy local or federal bureaucrat/thief may change the laws post your mortem? Lawyers get a bad rap. If you can find a good one, they're worth multiples of their fees.

Of course, it's all moot if you die broke.

Let's talk austerity budgets, nest eggs, and the power of compounding interest.

Single dudes love to spend, and why not? What's the point of haunting that office day in day out if not to buy yourself some kicks and goodies with your hard-earned gelt? Once you're a dad, you may want to throttle back on the impulse purchases. It matters not how much your income is—anyone can spend themselves into bankruptcy. Entertainers and athletes are especially good at it—think MC Hammer, Derek Sanderson, Burt Reynolds, Mike Tyson. (At his peak, it reputedly took $400,000 per month to maintain Iron Mike's lifestyle.)

People in the know say that two decades from now, the tab for four years at a top college will be in the neighborhood of $600k. And along the way, there are a myriad of expenses you just can't predict. Dance, voice, piano lessons. Orthodontics. Bail. Rehab. Gender reassignment surgery. You never know what the hell your kid will pull on you.

Is the local public elementary school graduating dunces and felons? These days, private elementary schools can run as high as $30,000 per year. (Yep, that's *elementary* school!) If you're self-employed, god knows how much you'll drop on medical insurance. Optimally, you'll be able to torque your income to keep pace, but still . . . if you'd like to cut spending, you can deploy a few tricks to ease the pain of cutting back.

First, remember it's all just *stuff* (see the Hellidays). Next, here are two proven techniques that dramatically curb spending.

Delayed Gratification

You're out and about and see the new Bentley/Riva/Vertu. You salivate. You reach for your wallet. STOP! Breathe deeply and count to ten. Then walk away. And stay away, for at least a week. In most cases, by the second day, thoughts of that purchase will have drifted from your mind, replaced by something else. (Gisele Bundchen's glutes?) How the hell to pay for such extravagant lunacy?

The X Factor

While at the beach with two pals, the topic turned to sunglasses. Joe had just bought a new pair of shades for an exorbitant (about $400) amount. Dave had also bought new sunglasses, for around $50. They tried each other's on, comparing and contrasting. There was a long silence, as Joe waited to hear how much more comfortable, glare-cutting and cool his shades were. Finally, Dave spoke. "Joe, your sunglasses are definitely better than mine. But not eight times better." We all laughed (even Joe) because it was so true.

The truth is, few premium-priced products are worth the premium price. In college I did some bartending, and we used to laugh like hell when some rube, in an attempt to impress his date, would order premium booze—in his mixed drink. *I'll have an Absolute and tonic,* he'd suavely request, eyebrow cocked like 007. Then we'd hand him some brand-x rot-gut vodka and snicker as he sipped and smacked his lips like a connoisseur.

There's a brand of wristwatch synonymous with status and success—probably the most counterfeited product on earth. Ask anybody who owns one—they're as accurate as a sundial at night. In fact, the fakes invariably keep better time because they have quartz movements, unlike the archaic (but quaint) mechanical movements of the genuine watches.

So when you're torn between a $7,500 wrist-chandelier/status symbol (that's not as accurate as a watch from a cereal box) and a timepiece costing one twentieth the price, it's a no-brainer, isn't it? Just calculate the X factor.

Is a $325,000 Maybach Benz 5 times better than a $60,000 Lexus? Prove it, Fritz.

Once you get in the habit of using delayed gratification and the X factor to evaluate your purchases, you'll be amazed how much more discretionary income you'll have. What to do with it?

If you're good with finance and have a solid grasp of the smorgasbord of available investments—and the time to closely monitor those investments—go to it. Or you can seek the help of a well-recommended financial planner. For starters, if your company offers a 401k or any type of profit-sharing plan, allocate as much of your income to it as possible.

Start a 529 college savings plan (so named for the IRS code) that lets you stockpile $$ tax-free until your kid's ready for college. This lets the interest compound a lot quicker. Most of the big investment houses offer them. T. Rowe Price explains it more clearly than most on their website, www.troweprice.com.

Life insurance is another dice roll to consider. If you die young, you want to leave a nice cash cushion behind, right? It all boils down to the same old chicken versus egg conundrum, *term versus whole*. It's morbid and mind-numbingly boring, but like tax returns and prostate exams, you gotta do it. Here's a valuable tip—talk to friends or a financial adviser *before* you contact any insurance salesmen, and know the policy you want going in. Those guys are like piranhas—once they get hold of you they never stop gnawing on you.

MACK STEPDADDY

If fatherhood is a marathon, being a stepfather must be like climbing Everest on roller blades. Dudes who buy into a pre-packaged family deserve awestruck admiration. It takes a special breed of cat to be a stepfather. It's one thing when your disobedient five-year-old contorts her face into a rictus of rage and hisses, *No, Daddy, I won't!* What must it feel like when some *other* guy's five-year-old does the same, adding, *and you're NOT my father!*

I have several friends who are stepdads, and they handle it adroitly. They tell me the number one hurdle is getting the child to like you. Whether the kid knew/knows his father or not, you are considered an interloper. It will take not weeks or months, but years until that child feels you deserve his respect and love.

Unless you and his mommy are in lockstep on every issue, you'll feel like the odd-man out in your own home. You must be in parallel agreement with her on every issue involving the child—meals, homework, TV, bedtime, treats, discipline, and so on. If he visits with his natural dad, you have to keep things cordial with him, too. You don't want him bad-mouthing you to the kid on alternate weekends.

Some stepdads try to buy their stepchild's affections, lavishing him with toys, ball games, and outings to amusement parks. It won't work. In fact, bribees immediately lose respect for the briber.

When hanging around with a stepdad and his kid, be extra mindful of his situation. I recall an incident with a pal whose seven-year-old stepdaughter was giving him a ration of shit. He sternly set her straight. I felt bad for the kid, and opened my big mouth with some ill-considered statement. My pal glared at me—"Don't undermine my authority," he said. I took no offense, because he was 100 percent right and I was 100 percent wrong. It took about ten years until I realized just how dumb I was, when a childless aunt pulled a worse stunt on me—offering to buy my daughter ice cream—two minutes after I'd sent her to her room for bad behavior.

Sometimes it takes a decade or more for a MACK STEPDADDY's generosity to pay a dividend. A friend who raised a stepdaughter from her early teens just attended her graduation from medical school. As she clutched her diploma and hugged him, she burst into tears. She apologized for all the undeserved flack she had given him over the years and acknowledged that her natural dad could and probably *would* not have sacrificed so she could have such a fabulous future. Ever the card, my pal asked, "Does this mean you'll waive the co-payment on my office visits?"

If It All Goes South

The odds of staying married are about 50 percent. Worse, a marriage is most likely to fail in the early years—when children are least able to cope with it. The most common reasons are financial problems, poor communication, infidelity, drugs/booze, and the various other abuses they tend to unleash. Until you're parents, it really doesn't matter *that* much. You get divorced, you find somebody else. But if you have kids, and you love them, you are linked to their mother for eternity. There never really is a divorce.

What if your happy home should be torn asunder by marital strife? Of course, the children get the worst of it. If it happens, a MACK DADDY's number one job is to minimize their suffering. Make no mistake about it—they *will* suffer—it's just a matter of degree and duration.

Once you and Mommy are certain the union is finished—separate ASAP. Kids are better off with one happy (or at least neutral) parent than two at war. Even infants pick up on domestic discord and hostile vibes. If over-exposed, it *will* damage them.

Some say the toughest part is masking emotions and squelching hostility. Divorced people who claim they're now "just good friends with the ex" are full of shit. What that cliché really means is they've managed to get their homicidal rage under control.

Lying sucks and it's stressful, but you really must act cordial when around the ex and the children. And, as difficult as it is, don't bad-mouth Mommy when she's not around. At a school picnic, I encountered a recently divorced couple. They had a boy and a girl, about four and six years of age. Since I'd last seen them, the boy had become quite blond. "Tommy must be out in the sun a lot," I remarked.

"Nah. He probably belongs to the mailman," was his dad's reply. Six-year-old Tommy may not have understood his father's exact meaning, but he sure as hell knew it wasn't good. And, the intended target of the insult—his ex-wife—was way out of earshot. Talk about your lose-lose situation.

Custody battles are brutal. Unless your ex-wife is a convicted serial killer, the courts will probably award her the kids—the laws are *that* biased against men.

Look at those reasons again—financial? You can always make more money. Poor communication? That can be improved. Infidelity? If you've strayed, or are thinking about it—think again and think of your children. Is their suffering worth some fleeting jollies? If she's the wanderer, is it possible to get past it and resume life? Alcoholism is not a disease, it's a choice—as is all drug abuse.

Divorce is a permanent, expensive, and emotionally devastating solution to problems that may be temporary and surmountable. Make it a last resort.

The Future

How did I get here . . . repeats on an endless loop in your mind. You stand in the back of the church and make lame jokes about *If my daughter had been a son I could have retired ten years ago . . . ha-ha.* People slap your back and shake your hand. On this bright spring morning, you don't really see, you just sort of make things out . . . as you would through glass bricks. Faces are blurred. Voices are muffled. Maybe this is just a dream. Maybe you'll awaken and trip on one of her pull toys as you get out of bed.

Somebody, please start a leaf blower or let the phone ring . . . just wake me, please.

Christ, don't let a tear leak out of my eye and give me away. I'm supposed to be happy for her. You swallow but cannot shift the tennis ball lodged in your throat. Your wife shoots you a look from across the vestibule. Did her expression say *what's wrong* or *buck up?* She's always had an irrational fear of you having a coronary—are you about to turn her fear into a premonition?

You hear the sound of the church organ and curse yourself for feeling the way you do, but your sorrow is . . . *unbearable.* You've weathered some heavy storms—that near-death experience as a teenager in the car wreck. You sat with your dad (and fought back tears) when he got . . . the prognosis. You held your mom in your arms as she died. But this . . . this is tougher than any of them. Your baby . . . your fat little burbling baby, your wobbly legged toddler, your pig-tailed first grader, your skinny-legged 11-year-old, your tinsel-toothed teenaged rock diva, your Magna Cum Laude graduate all-grown-up in her cap and gown . . . is leaving you. *What's that goddamn quotation—your greatest fear shall be realized? Well, here it is.* And you're throwing a huge party to celebrate the saddest moment in your life to date.

You've been to a lot of weddings. A lot of funerals, too. It's strange how similar they are. *Hey, I gotta stop this. This is a wedding, not a funeral.* You try to think of other rationalizations as to why you should be happy. They're not flowing.

Worst of all, you have to smile and play a part in this idiotic tableau—walk her down the aisle and "give her away" to him.

Not that he's a bad guy. He seems okay. But who is worthy of her? *NO ONE, THAT'S WHO!*

That jerky usher with the bad toupee nudges you. You turn and see her. *Oh my God, she looks like my wife did that day* . . . she is so incredibly beautiful and she is so . . . happy. She smiles her trillion-watt smile and hugs you. *Oh, sweet Jesus, please . . . PLEASE don't let me come unglued now!* You break the clinch and pull it together. The tennis ball deflates and the tears are miraculously siphoned back into their ducts.

Only yesterday you stooped to hold her tiny hand when you crossed the street. Now, she takes your arm as the organist revs up "Here Comes the Bride."

You walk with her.

She double-squeezes your arm . . . the same signal you used to give her that meant *don't be afraid . . . I'm with you.*

She knows . . .

Seems we were just laughing about epidurals and here we are at the epilogue. It all went by so fast.

Does the scene depicted above seem light-years away? It isn't. And if you get to partake in it—ball in throat, tears in eyes and all—you'll be one very lucky MACK DADDY. A fairly hefty percentage of guys expire before their daughters marry.

If nothing else, believe this: *Tempus Fugit*. The years will whip by like fence posts on a freeway. Your son or daughter will grow and be gone. If you think you've felt a void in your heart before, it will be a pinhole in comparison to the crater your child will create when she leaves home.

Your baby will always be your *baby*. Regardless of your child's accomplishments, she will be your *baby*. Whether Pulitzer or Nobel Prize–winner, corporate titan, entrepreneurial phenomenon, outlaw biker, butcher, baker, or candlestick maker—your *baby*.

You will never, ever love anyone with the ferocity with which you love your child. And therefore, no person wields the power to shatter your heart as your child could. This is your most important relationship—treat it as if your life depended on it.

If you're reading this book, odds are you're a new dad or about to become one. Let's close the karmic loop.

If you have a baby, hold it now.

Close your eyes.

Open your mind.

Watch the images slowly dissolve from one to another.

See your baby crawl, walk, talk, laugh, cry, rage, go to school, run, stumble, fall, and rise.

See her riding a bike, driving, holding a diploma, working, throwing a bouquet.

See her with her own kids.

See her with gray in her hair, sitting quietly, looking at a faded picture of the two of you.

Hear her whisper, *Daddy.*

Is she smiling her trillion-watt smile?

If so, you were one hell of a MACK DADDY.